Feminizing Politics

For Alan

Feminizing Politics

Joni Lovenduski

polity

First published in 2005 by Polity Press

Polity Press
65 Bridge Street
Cambridge CB2 1UR, UK

Polity Press
350 Main Street
Malden, MA 02148, USA

ISBN 0 7456 2462 6
ISBN 0 7456 2463 4 (paperback)

A catalogue record for this book is available from the British Library
and has been applied for from the Library of Congress.

Typeset in 11 on 13pt Sabon
by Graphicraft Limited, Hong Kong
Printed and bound in Great Britain by TJ International Ltd,
Padstow, Cornwall

For further information on Polity, visit our website: www.polity.co.uk

Contents

Acknowledgements   vi

List of Tables   viii

List of Abbreviations   ix

Chapter 1   Introduction   1

Chapter 2   Feminism and Political Representation:
            Ideas and Struggles   12

Chapter 3   Obstacles to Feminizing Politics   45

Chapter 4   Equality Strategies and the Quota
            Movement   83

Chapter 5   Examples: Quotas and *Parité*   105

Chapter 6   Making a Difference? Conclusions   140

References   181

Index   190

v

Acknowledgements

Any mistakes in *Feminizing Politics* are mine. Its achievements are the result of the array of debts I incurred in the process of writing it. Louise Knight and Andrea Drugan at Polity were helpful and efficient. They waited a long time for a manuscript that was repeatedly put aside as I changed jobs, moved house and dealt with crises of various kinds. Deborah Lincoln and Meg Russell helped not only with information but also patiently explained to me what was wrong with many of my insights into Labour Party politics. Fiona MacKay responded generously to repeated requests for information about Scotland. Sarah Childs made the manuscript of *Women Representing Women: New Labour's Women MPs* available to me, and Mona Lena Krook allowed me to read and cite unpublished papers that are part of her forthcoming doctoral thesis – all acts of great generosity. Rainbow Murray explained the intricacies of the French electoral system. My former colleague Paul Hirst encouraged me to believe the book was worthwhile. I continue to miss him. My colleagues at Birkbeck offered the stimulating and supportive environment that I needed to complete the manuscript. Participants in the RNGS project (Research Network on Gender, Politics and the State) kept me focused on political representation

Acknowledgements

issues. Dionyssis Dimitrakopoulos provided emergency reading on institutionalism. Rodney Barker and Alan Ware kindly read and commented on the original draft. Two anonymous readers made extensive comments that were constructive and helpful. I am especially grateful for the advice to rewrite chapter 5. I did so. While writing the book I was fortunate enough to be supervising Rosie Campbell, Rainbow Murray and Rosemary Taylorson, graduate students whose work made me rethink many of my arguments and claims. The research on candidates that is reported in several chapters is based on two joint projects. I worked with Pippa Norris of Harvard University on the British Representation Study 2001, which was funded by Harvard University, and with Laura Shepherd Robinson, then at Fawcett, on a study of women who sought selection in the 2001 UK general election. The Fawcett study was funded by the Nuffield Foundation small grants scheme. Rainbow Murray proofread the final draft. Throughout the process, Alan Ware offered intellectual support and criticism, kindness, the great patience that it takes to live with me when I am writing and large quantities of dry white wine. I am grateful to them all.

List of Tables

5.1 Labour women MPs and candidates,
    1979–1992   117
5.2 Women and men elected to the Scottish
    Parliament 1999, by party and type of seat   125
5.3 Women and men elected to the Welsh
    Assembly 1999, by party and type of seat   125
5.4 Women's representation as a percentage
    of party representation in UK political
    institutions, 2003   129
5.5 Post-*parité* electoral outcomes: National
    Assembly elections, 2002   134

List of Abbreviations

AM	Assembly Member
AWS	All-Women Shortlist
CEDAW	Convention on the Elimination of Discrimination Against Women
EMILY	Early Money is Like Yeast
EOC	Equal Opportunities Commission
GLA	Greater London Assembly
IPU	Inter Parliamentary Union
LWAC	Labour Women's Action Committee
LWN	Labour Women's Network
NEC	National Executive Committee (Labour Party)
MP	Member of Parliament
MSF	Manufacturing, Science and Finance
MSP	Member of the Scottish Parliament
PLP	Parliamentary Labour Party
PPS	Parliamentary Private Secretary
RPR	Rally for the Republic
SNP	Scottish National Party
UNIFEM	United Nations Development Fund for Women
WNC	Women's National Commission

1

Introduction

In Vera Brittain's novel, *The Honourable Estate*, Ruth Alleyndene is a political activist selected to stand as a Labour Party candidate just after British women won full suffrage in 1928. She enters Parliament in 1929. The novel gives no picture of parliamentary life. But it does describe the thinking behind her selection. Alleyndene was a prominent local activist. In this fictionalized account, the rising Labour Party makes opportunistic use of her name and her sex to attract the votes of newly enfranchised women. Her talents include a good education and an ability for public speaking and to argue from a woman's perspective, examples of which are carefully described in the novel. Brittain's depiction reflects her belief – and that of many of her contemporaries – that women would be selected by parties as candidates once they were enfranchised. The expectation was that parties would be feminized, would include more women and would take more account of women's interests.

In fact, British political parties did not select women for winnable seats in substantial numbers until the mid-1990s, almost 90 years after they were first enfranchised. As a result, elected institutions did not become feminized. Nor did most important appointed institutions. Wherever decisions were made and power might be thought to be present, women were excluded.

Feminists and their opponents have consistently held unrealistic expectations of the possibilities afforded by real systems of political representation. Over the years since women were enfranchised, the meanings of their political action and of political representation changed; however, reactions both by traditionalists and by many feminists did not take such changes into account. Although expectations of women representatives are unrealistic, the impact of feminists on public policy has actually been underestimated. In short, both the possibilities and the achievements of women's political representation have been misunderstood.

Moreover, feminists are divided about political representation. Women's political action is understood in terms of two contradictory perspectives in feminist thought. For the sake of brevity I will label them 'equality' and 'difference' feminism. Equality feminism (sometimes termed 'equity' or 'liberal' feminism) stresses women's entitlements to be in politics on the same terms and in the same numbers as men. Difference feminism (sometimes termed 'maternal' or 'social' feminism) stresses that women have particular characteristics or interests and perspectives that may be represented only by women. For many critics the first position implies that women representatives will become political men; the second, that women representatives will change the practice and nature of politics. Both positions inform attitudes to women and politics and also impressions of what women do as politicians. Both the critics and the supporters of women's political representation tend to elide the two positions.

The tendency to elide equality and difference arguments is intertwined with misunderstandings of the nature of political institutions and is especially evident in commentary on recent British politics. On the one hand, women politicians are criticized for their failure to transform centuries-old male-designed traditions of politics. On the other hand, women MPs are expected to represent a particular model of womanhood – they are frequently either credited with bringing significant changes in policy that are supportive of women's traditional family roles, or blamed for not doing so. The two bases of judgement, one derived from principles of equity and the other from ideas about difference, parallel justifications for women's representation. They are contradictory and seem compatible with each other only because they come from separate intellectual communities, tend not to be confronted together and are rarely spelled out in detail.

What are the implications of the contradiction? The two kinds of judgement bear directly on women politicians and are a constant pressure on them. Equity arguments expose women representatives to assessment on the basis of inappropriate 'male' criteria. To perform effectively, women politicians are expected to conform to the rules of the game. By contrast, the difference justification of women's representation and the maternalist thrust of expectations of policy impacts risk locking political women into traditional family roles at the very moment that such roles are undergoing profound change. Arguably, British political institutions, with their deeply embedded traditional characteristics, have been especially insulated from the impact of major changes in gender relations. However, it is fair to say that political institutions in general are good at protecting their cultures and procedures.

Understanding the processes of increasing women's representation requires us to keep both equity and difference perspectives in play. Women representatives operate in a context in which expectations are insensitive not only to sex and gender differences, but also to the constraints of different political arenas, cultures and processes or of the real achievements that have resulted from feminist interventions in politics. A complex set of beliefs about what should happen obscures a complex political reality.

The interplay of equality and difference considerations frames much of the thinking behind the organization of this book. If women politicians are to make no difference, then why should we support them? But if change is expected to result from the presence of women, then women will be obliged to produce change, probably over a very short time span, which is exactly what is difficult to do in established political systems. When change is not forthcoming, the new women politicians will be accused of failure and betrayal.

To think through this difficult situation we need to have an appreciation of political processes and outcomes. Thus feminists have interrogated theories of representation, rebuilding such theories to include concerns of women's equality. Ironically, that project contributes to the expectation that changes in the numbers of women in politics will bring changes not only in the results of representation but also in its processes. In the jargon of representation theory, descriptive representation will lead to substantive representation (Phillips 1995). Such arguments evoke Cockburn's (1991) call for a vision of equal opportunities policy in which a 'short agenda' of anti-discrimination measures leads to a 'long agenda' of a transformation of gender relations. In politics the short agenda of increasing women's presence leads to a long agenda of political transformation (Mackay 2001).

These arguments have considerable appeal. But the expectations they create produce conditions in which new women politicians are condemned to disappoint their supporters and provide ammunition for their many opponents. Often opponents incorporate hopes for change (that they do not themselves share) into their attacks. In the introduction to her book, *Women Representing Women* (2004a), Sarah Childs details the press reaction to the election of 101 Labour Party women to the House of Commons in 1997. The increase in the numbers of women was one of the big stories of the election. They were presented on the one hand as harbingers of change, but on the other as 'Blair's Babes', criticized (often in terms of some cruelty) for their alleged lack of fashion sense, for their behaviour and for not making a difference from day one.

What they were actually doing on day one and during the first few months of the new Parliament was getting organized in their new jobs, as were all the other new MPs. The initial unpleasantness became set-piece stories that recurred frequently in the first parliamentary year. As time went by the sniping accelerated as women attempted to introduce changes. For example, when they tried and failed to get the Speaker's permission to breastfeed in the House of Commons, they were accused of being unprofessional (*Guardian*, 15 April 2000). The tone of commentary was destructive. Where the content of a press report might be even-handed, the sub-editor ensured that the activities of women MPs were trivialized (see for example, 'Blair's Babes at Westminster say the House is no place for mothers', *Sunday Telegraph*, 21 May 2000). Unpleasantness became a feeding frenzy at the end of 1997 when new women MPs failed to rebel against the party in a vote on an issue of special concern to women. Only one new Labour woman MP, Ann Cryer, was among the 47 who voted against the Social Security Bill that included a reduction in benefits paid to lone parents (almost all of whom are women). From that point vilification accelerated as, triumphantly, commentators proclaimed the failure of the new women MPs.

The pattern of criticism described by Childs is a fairly typical example of backlash, of resistance to change in a gender regime. The number of women in the House of Commons was not large, but it was larger than ever before. The proportion of women MPs doubled in 1997 to around 18 per cent of the House of Commons and 24 per cent of the Parliamentary Labour Party. This change, far short of balanced representation of women and men, was quite different from previous breaches of parliamentary maleness. For example, two decades previously, Margaret Thatcher was able to become leader of the Conservative Party and later the first woman prime minister, with considerable support from male MPs *because* of her rarity. As historian Linda Colley observed: 'she was not a precedent. There were no groups of others like her "queuing up to follow"' (Colley 2000). Thatcher did not portend a danger to the established gender regime of politics. Indeed, she never appointed another elected woman to her cabinet during three successive terms of office. Not only was she a token, she was a special kind of token: a queen bee. By contrast, despite their minority status, the group of Labour women MPs after 1997 threatened the end of the 'token woman' at Westminster and portended major changes (Colley 2000). There were, and are, others queuing up behind. Moreover the queues are forming across the party system and throughout the political apparatus.

Before going on to explain the structure of this book, I want to say something more about the issue of equality and difference. When I first thought about writing this book in the late 1990s, I was interested in revisiting equality and difference arguments in the context of women's political representation. Some five years later it had become clear to me that that work has been done. Good accounts of the politics of equality and difference feminisms have been written by scholars who explore the arguments attending each formulation. Many argue that difference feminism should be revisited and revalued. Such accounts are most effective when they take account of the context in which feminist actors must operate. Five examples have particularly impressed me. Jane Freedman (2001) explores the evolution of feminist theory from the standpoint of equality and difference. Fiona Mackay (2001) finds strong evidence for a version of the politics of care in the 'common sense' of women politicians. Sarah Childs (2004a) has researched the experiences, attitudes and styles of new Labour women MPs to consider if they 'act for' women. Hilary Footit (2002) identifies a 'women's' language of politics that is distinct from men's in ways that reflect the concerns of difference feminism. Lynne E. Ford (2001) describes the politics of women's equality in the USA using distinctions between difference and equality feminism as her organizing concepts. These very successful studies argue from qualitative evidence that some women bring new concerns to the political agenda and suggest that women politicians have altered the political discourse. All acknowledge that their studies are institutionally specific.

It is likely that the phenomena they describe are also temporally specific, moments, sometimes rather long moments, in a history of change at a time of transition both in political life more generally and in gender relations. In the same way that gender relations shape state institutions, even at moments of major change, so also are gender relations shaped by political institutions. When mobilizations to claim women's representation coincide with other changes, sources of transformation may quickly be obscured. We therefore need to disentangle the various processes to assess their effects.

Recent feminist research captures the change in state institutions. In general, over the period in which women's political representation has expanded, changes have taken place both in the structures of states and in gender relations. States have offloaded some capacities to quasi-state organizations, downloaded others to regional units and uploaded others to international organizations in processes that were affected by women's movements (Banaszak et al. 2003). In industrialized democracies demographic change and patterns of increased women's employment and education led to changes in gender relations and increased possibilities of autonomy for women. Established political institutions slowly began to catch up as governments started to include more women politicians in high office.

Such inclusion appears to vary. The patterns of political representation with which we now live were first apparent in the Scandinavian states, where the proportions of women in politics began to increase in the 1980s. Scholars who tracked the progress of women through Scandinavian institutions have closely examined these patterns. Their studies show that, while women remain in a minority, there are two common features to their position as representatives. Both are visible in British politics. First, there is a persistent pattern of decreasing numbers of women representatives the further up the decision-making hierarchy one looks. Second, a functional division of labour between women and men representatives is present in many systems. Women are more likely to specialize in 'soft' and less prestigious policy areas such as health, cultural affairs, education and social welfare, while men dominate the traditionally more prestigious areas of economic management, foreign affairs and home affairs (Karvonen and Selle 1995; Bergqvist et al. 1999). The fact that health, education and social welfare consume so much public expenditure and are so important to the daily lives of citizens has yet to alter the old-world hierarchies of government functions.

Two opposing perspectives have been suggested to explain these divisions. On the one hand it is claimed that there is an 'iron law' of politics in which the proportions of women decrease as the hierarchy of power is ascended. The 'iron law' is a restatement of women's exclusion. On the other hand it is argued that new mobilizations of voters take time to establish a presence in decision-making hierarchies. The implication here is that women will catch up in high office only after they have been present in intermediate positions for some time. Known as the 'lag' hypothesis, this view posits that a pool of eligibles must become established at each level of a hierarchy before the next level can be ascended. When the 'lag' hypothesis and the 'iron law' are combined, the notion of 'shrinking institutions' is sometimes introduced, which suggests that women ascend the political hierarchy only as and when its institutions become less important. It operates as an indicator of the importance of the office that is being examined. If women are present, then the office must be relatively less important than those held by men (Karvonen and Selle 1995).

The Scandinavian research alerts us to the realization that women representatives will expect to encounter barriers to power at all levels of the political hierarchy. The work by Banaszak and her colleagues (2003) describes a political world of moving goalposts and shifting sites of power. Recent scholarship on gender and the state therefore suggests a universe of important, complex institutions in which the quality of political representation is affected by the entry of women. It underlines how important it is that assessments of women's representation are sensitive to such institutional realities.

Women's presence may affect the language of politics. Scandinavian research has shown that a new political discourse that reflects women's concerns may become a generalized political language (Dahlerup 1988). There are at least two reasons for this. First, male politicians may adopt languages and issues that enable them to appeal to the whole electorate and, second, generation change may bring men with less traditional attitudes into politics. Here is an example of combined processes that are difficult to disentangle. It is also difficult to separate feminist from other effects, a problem made worse by the divided nature of feminism.

However, it is possible to describe the institutional and cultural settings in which debates about women's political representation are located and to trace their progress through successive political cycles. By locating and tracing arguments about women's political representation in their institutional settings, the way that expectations of women representatives have developed may be demonstrated. It is possible in this way to show how the constraints of real political situations affect the capacities of actually existing women politicians and vice versa.

Accordingly, in this book I explore the process, the threats and portents of increasing the numbers of women in political representation. I discuss the arguments that are made for and against women's claims for equal political representation. I pose the question of what else happens when the number of women changes.

This book is mainly about the processes of achieving increases in the political representation of British women, but it also takes account of comparative trends and especially of the growing use of quotas as a means to secure women's representation. The cause of both the 1997 'breakthrough' and the queue of women that accompanied it was the implementation of quotas of women by the Labour Party.

Introduction

Between 1993 and 1996 the Labour Party operated a system of all-women shortlists to guarantee the selection of women candidates for winnable seats in the coming election. Without that device the numbers of elected women would have been much lower (Eagle and Lovenduski 1998). The politics of that decision, of its overturning and its eventual reinstatement are discussed in detail in chapter 5 of this book. I draw attention to it here because I wish to point out that whilst of great importance, it was not, comparatively speaking, an unusual decision. Quotas of women, apparently so exotic in the circles of British politics, became a commonplace arrangement for candidate selection during the 1990s. However, debates about how to secure women's representation continue in British politics, where the method has many staunch opponents.

This book is intended to be an intervention in those debates. Its aims are, first, to rehearse the arguments for equality of political representation of women and men; second, to describe and explain the movements and arrangements to increase women's political representation in Britain; third, to place British developments in a wider context, drawing attention to similar developments in other countries and regions of the world. The fourth aim is to demonstrate the continuing importance of institutions to the nature of and possibilities for political representation. Finally, I aim once again to draw the attention of political scientists to the importance of gender to the study of politics. I hope this intervention will not only inform and extend discussion of the methods that best achieve equality of women's representation and provide resources for its advocates, but also add to the pressure to incorporate gender into the mainstream of political science.

My approach is discursive. Although my latest research is presented here, this book is not a conventional academic monograph. It is an exploration of how to think about the feminization of politics. The context is one in which claims by women for presence are more frequent, more widespread and more effective, in which positive discrimination policies are proliferating and in which at least a few countries have experienced balanced political representation of women and men. I argue that to understand the feminization of politics it is necessary to understand the institutions in which the processes are taking place. My exploration breaks down into a set of questions that parallel representative processes. In chapter 2, I discuss what is meant by feminizing politics, how feminists have engaged in politics and why we might expect women to make a difference. In chapter 3, I consider the obstacles to increasing the number of women in politics, looking mainly at the British example. Chapter 4 outlines strategies that have been used to overcome those obstacles. Chapter 5 extends that discussion to an account of the adoption of quotas in Britain and France. Chapter 6 discusses the effects of feminizing politics and concludes by revisiting the question of what else happens when the number of women increases.

2

Feminism and Political Representation: Ideas and Struggles

The first step in this exploration of feminizing politics is to clarify the terms of the enquiry. The meanings of politics, feminism, representation and interests are various and subject to considerable selection and interpretation. Therefore, what follows are my preferred selections and interpretations. In this chapter I lay the foundations for the remainder of the book. First, I define terms and explain the concepts that I intend to use. Second, I describe, very briefly, the claims of feminist movements for the political representation of women.

Politics

I start with a definition of politics. Politics is a concept that is both difficult and contested. In its taken-for-granted everyday usage, politics conjures images of politicians, assemblies, governments and elections often framed as gladiatorial competitions or races by a media that is a necessary part of the process. The term is suggestive and frequently negative, implying something opaque, hidden, unsavoury, treacherous and dangerous. Thus feminizing politics is the insertion and integration of women, both in terms of numbers and ideas, into a process that is important but widely considered to be unappealing.

For those interested in women's roles in mainstream politics it is necessary to work not only with popular meanings of the term 'politics' but also with the diffuse nature of what, for feminists, constitutes the political. Although these meanings require extensive treatment, more than can be offered in this brief volume, they must be kept in play. I propose here a definition of politics that describes how the term will be used in this book. Politics consists of the personnel, processes, relationships, institutions and procedures that make authoritative public decisions. Not everything that everyone might consider to be political is included in my description, but it has the advantage that almost everyone would agree that all of what is included is political.

For feminists, the political encompasses personal and private (domestic) life, which is predicated on unequal power relations in which men have more power than women and also have power over women. Arguably, in terms of gender, political institutions mirror private institutions. That politics is male-dominated has long been well known. However, recently the presence of women in public political institutions has grown and that growth is accompanied by rising interest in what it portends. As commonly formulated, the question of what difference more women in politics will make asks whether the increased presence of women will transform democratic politics. This question animates contemporary debate on women and politics. It is a complicated question that touches on a number of core political concerns. It may very well not be answerable. But it may be possible to make some progress toward an answer by exploring what is involved, in real political institutions, spelling out the underlying assumptions of the question and considering its component parts. That is the project of this book.

Two assumptions underpin my understanding of feminizing politics. First, a significant element of the roles women and men play in politics depends not only on each other but also on the nature of institutions of political representation. Representative institutions determine the processes of feminizing politics. Second, the way feminists think about political representation is at least as important as how the processes actually operate. It is feminist theory that illuminates the gendered nature of political representation.

To justify those two assumptions, in the remainder of this chapter I assemble the main ideas and concepts that support them. First, I examine the idea of political representation and how it relates to women. Second, I consider the political dimensions of feminist ideas and, finally, I discuss the interplay of both, using examples from women's movement mobilizations for representation and citizenship.

The Idea of Political Representation

The political representation of a group can be understood as the presence of members of the group in the formal institutions of politics. The theory, at its simplest, is that representatives act for the groups they represent. However, in representative democracies most of those who are elected to the legislatures act for many different groups and most also attempt to transcend specific or narrow group interests to act for the nation or community that the institution serves. For example, an MP may act for her political party, her constituency, her region, her nation and her ethnic group, while also seeking to balance different viewpoints within an overall understanding of the 'national' interest. The multi-dimensional nature of representation complicates arguments for women's representation. Political representation theory suggests that representatives have an incentive to represent the interests of those who voted for them or who might vote for them in the future even though they themselves do not share that interest. In such a formulation the election acts as a perfect market in which all political demands are cleared. Hence it should not matter who the representatives are. In practice, elections do not work like that. Most representatives tend to represent interests that they do not share only if they constitute a large, coherent, self-conscious minority in the community. Otherwise many interests will be ignored. As we shall see shortly, women are not a cohesive group, so this argument that men could represent them scarcely works at all.

The practice of political representation is institutionally specific. By this I mean that the forms it takes and its importance depend on where it is sited. The idea, however, is abstract and general. The institutional specificity of processes of feminizing politics is well illustrated by the British case. Here, arguments in favour of equal representation of women come from three main sources: first, the general principles of representative democracy modified to the liberal democratic framework of the constitution; second, the system of party government; and third, feminist advocacy. Only feminist advocates give first priority to sex equality in political representation. Such advocates draw on the principles of democratic representation and intervene in party politics to make claims for equality between men and women. When women struggled to win the right to vote, they imagined that with the vote would come women's representation, an expectation that was not met. Until 1997 women constituted fewer than 10 per cent of members of the House of Commons (MPs). Between 1918 and 1983 fewer than 5 per cent of MPs were women. The pattern of underrepresentation persisted despite women's growing achievements in education, work and other areas of public life and despite growing numbers of qualified women seeking political office. Inevitably, British women began to mobilize to seek political equality. At the end of the 1970s, equality of representation again became an important part of the women's agenda and by the end of the 1980s a widespread movement for political equality had emerged. By the end of the 1990s such demands appeared to be inescapable, as growing numbers of women entered active politics.

Feminism and Political Representation

Why is equality of women's representation important? At the heart of this question is the issue of whether women need women to represent them. Until fairly recently it was thought that women were perfectly adequately represented by male heads of household and the notion that women might have different interests from their families was not widely considered. However, as social patterns have changed, it has become easier to agree that women have rights as citizens that entitle them to participate in government, where those interests can be defended and advanced. This 'claim of right' has been an important feature of the mobilization of British women.

Issues of women's representation are both illuminated and obscured by debates about the nature of representation. Hannah Pitkin famously expressed its complexity when she wrote: 'representation, taken generally, means the making present in some sense of something which is nevertheless not present, literally or in fact' (1967: 8–9). By definition then, representative democracy institutionalizes *limited* participation. In short, the idea of representative democracy does not necessarily support claims for inclusion. Representation is not even necessarily associated with democracy. The key institutions in which British political representation takes place pre-dated representative democracy. However, David Judge argues that British political institutions were unable to accommodate popular sovereignty. This sequence is important because it suggests that pre-existing institutions were not sufficiently adapted to take account of democratic functions. As a result, discussion of political representation in Britain is 'replete with paradoxes' in which common assumptions about the democratic nature of the system are not expressed in its institutional arrangements. Moreover, British political practice is not only specific, and imperfectly democratic, it is often peculiar (Judge 1999: 19–20). Even in this eccentric system, however, there are some common basic concerns with the quality of political representation.

Descriptive Representation

Democratic theorists distinguish between substantive and descriptive representation. The claim that women should be present in decision-making in proportion to their membership of the population is a claim for descriptive representation (sometimes called proportionate, pictorial or microcosmic representation). Calls for the descriptive representation of women propose that women should represent women in proportion to their presence in the population. Such claims challenge systems of representation in which groups of the population are consistently excluded from representative assemblies and committees. 'In descriptive representation, representatives are in their own persons and lives in some sense typical of the larger class of persons whom they represent' (Mansbridge 1999). Thus women legislators represent women, black legislators represent black people and so forth. The term 'descriptive representation' may also be used to capture particular experiences; for example, where it is thought that farmers are needed to represent farmers (Mansbridge 1999). However, it raises the prospect of claims by any number of groups, which is one of the main criticisms of opponents of measures to ensure the proportionate presence of women in politics.

On the basis that descriptive representation is impractical and undesirable, its opponents make three arguments. First, they draw attention to the difficulty for any system of meeting claims by all possible component groups. In Britain the criticism that claims for descriptive representation are impracticable ignores the existing biases of the system against women or ethnic minorities, while paradoxically implying that such biases cannot be lessened (Judge 1999). What of its undesirability? Responding to claims by women for inclusion, they point out that the claims of other, smaller, possibly more 'deserving' or 'oppressed' groups, such as minority groups, have a stronger basis for claims than women. In this way the arguments for descriptive representation lead to pressure on feminists to take responsibility for the representation of other excluded groups. The answer to this criticism is that political movements establish which categories warrant pro-portionate representation (Phillips 1995: 61; Judge 1999: 44). Finally, those who argue that descriptive representation is undesirable assert that the job of representative necessarily requires skills that are not uniformly distributed in the popula-tion. Their case is that to insist on proportionate representa-tion on the basis of social characteristics risks the selection of unenlightened decision-makers. This argument, in its support for the status quo, entails that whiteness and maleness, char-acteristic of most British legislators to date, are prerequisites of competence (Judge 1999: 45).

Substantive Representation

The concept of substantive representation captures the content of the decisions of representatives. The substantive representation of a group is most simply described as the representation of its interests. In many political situations the representation of one's interest may be more important than the representation of one's kind. Thus, after the first post-women's suffrage elections, feminists may have preferred to vote for supporters of feminist causes, whatever their sex, than to vote for women who did not support feminist causes. However, this is not a cut-and-dried case. Contempor-ary feminists argue that the very presence of a woman in a legislature is important for changing its culture and priorities and especially for increasing its range of concerns.

Women's interests

Substantive representation turns on the idea of interest. The identification of interest is controversial in politics. It raises major questions of what a group's interests are, how they may be known and who is entitled to recognize and identify them. Can we say that *women*, who are a diverse group possibly sharing only their historic underrepresentation and potential reproductive capacity, have common interests to be represented?

The difficult question of women's interests has long exercised feminists who have repeatedly debated their nature (Sapiro 1981). To move beyond those debates, some authors have suggested a distinction between women's issues and women's perspectives (Lovenduski 1997). Women's issues may be thought of as issues that mainly affect women, either for biological reasons (for example, breast cancer screening) or for social reasons (sex equality or childcare policy). Women's perspectives, however, are women's views on all political concerns. Many analysts argue that, although men and women agree that broadly the same issues are significant, women perceive those issues differently. For example, Fawcett Society research in the mid-1990s found that while both women and men prioritized economic issues, women were more concerned about part-time work, low pay and pension rights, while men were more worried about unemployment (Lovenduski 1997; Stephenson 1998).

Within feminist scholarship and advocacy, with their bases in difference and equality, the problem of defining interests is compounded. On the one hand, affirming the diversity of women with their varying interests is a central concern of contemporary feminist theory. Feminist theory scrupulously recognizes that class, race, ethnicity, sexuality, physical ability, marital status, motherhood and religion divide women and are important sources of identities and interests. Such divisions inevitably lead to conflicts of interest, to competitive claims from different groups. On the other hand, effective political mobilization requires shared recognition of common interests. To be effective politically, feminists are required to relax their insistence on difference, thus undermining one of their central concerns.

These difficulties of placing women and women's interests into mainstream theories of political representation are indicative of the complexity of the project of integrating women into political discourse. First it was necessary to show how women had been excluded from politics and to consider the implications of such exclusion. Gradually feminist scholarship detailed and explained the absence of women from politics, a project largely completed by the end of the 1980s. For many scholars the turning point was the publication of Carole Pateman's *The Sexual Contract* in 1988. Pateman's book was a watershed, after which there was a shift of emphasis to the implications of inclusion (Mansbridge 1999; Phillips 1999) and discussion of the integration of women became a major project of scholarship. In the process, the analysis of women's political condition was increasingly informed by the interdisciplinary approaches of the women's studies movement. To explain this point, it is necessary to make some further distinctions.

Sex and Gender

The distinction between sex and gender illuminates differences among women and among men. Although research shows some differences of attitude and preference *between* women and men, if we look beneath this surface we also quickly find major differences *among* women and *among* men. Feminists have sought to analyse such differences by considering the effects of both sex and gender on politics. This important distinction has been much elaborated. Gender is not a synonym for sex. Moreover, both concepts are contested. During the 1990s feminist theorists questioned the usefulness of the sex–gender distinction. They argued that both sex and gender should be understood as performance and that neither biological nor social distinctions between women and men or between masculinity and femininity could be sustained.

This understanding suggests the power of institutions in shaping masculinity and femininity (Lovenduski 1998). In short, there are different and competing ways of thinking about this important distinction that imply different ways of thinking about political interests. Most simply, sex is a biological category that separates men and women. Gender is the set of social meanings attached to the categories of male and female. Another way of conceptualizing gender is to think of it as a scale of attributes ranging from masculinity to femininity. Women are more likely than men to possess feminine attributes, but such attributes do not belong exclusively to women. The same point may be made about men and masculinity. Gender also expresses the effects of relationships between women and men and of relationships among women and among men. These relationships are manifested in differences of political power, social roles, images and expectations, resulting in recognized characteristics of masculinity and femininity that differ over time and across cultures. Thus gender is a set of attributes and a process. The concept suggests a changing contextualized social, psychological and political phenomenon which affects the way groups of women and men define their interests.

The fact that women's interests are at least as diverse as those of men is itself a basis for claiming equality of political representation. However, real claims for women's representation tend to invoke arguments that are resonant in the particular political arrangements in which advocates are working. Feminist theory is a source of their arguments, but likely to be much adapted. Normally, in modern democracies, claims for women's political representation are first framed in the dichotomous terms of sex difference, expressed as absolute differences between women and men. Arguably, as understandings of sex and gender become more widespread, that framing changes to include a language of gender difference in which problems are considered in terms of similarities and differences among women and men (Stetson 2002).

Arguments for Equality of Representation

There are at least three types of argument put forward to support claims for women's representation: justice arguments, pragmatic arguments and difference arguments.

Justice arguments

Perhaps the most powerful arguments in favour of increased women's representation are those based on principles of justice. These arguments claim that it is simply unfair for men to monopolize representation, especially in a country that considers itself a modern democracy. Anne Phillips states: 'There is no argument from justice that can defend the current state of affairs; and . . . there *is* an argument from justice for parity between women and men' (1995: 65). Additional arguments about the nature of representation may obscure this central point, but they can never overturn it. The justice argument is also supported by claims from citizenship. Citizenship is the set of rights, duties, attachments and identities that constitute one's belonging to the political system. In constitutional terms, women formally have equal citizenship to men in democratic systems. However, the way in which citizenship is defined by institutional arrangements may have different effects on women and men. The narrowly conceived British democracy described above permits an electoral system that is particularly unfavourable to women. Arguably, the Westminster electoral system is a major obstacle to women's representation (Vallance 1979).

Pragmatic arguments

Pragmatic arguments draw on notions of vote-maximizing rational politicians. This case is based on the advantages to political parties of increasing their numbers of women representatives. Proponents highlight the importance of women's votes in terms of electoral success. For example, British sex equality advocates point to the long-standing gender gap in voting whereby women were more likely than men to vote for the Conservative Party. The traditional gender gap gave disproportionate electoral success to the Conservative Party, which dominated government during the twentieth century. Had women voted in the same way as men, there would have been no Conservative governments between 1945 and 1979.

Advocates of pragmatic arguments advance the claim that women are more likely to vote for parties that elect women candidates. They draw on difference arguments to contend that women have, and know they have, particular experiences and interests, which can only be understood and represented by women. They argue that masculine party images are old-fashioned and unattractive to women voters. According to this logic, recent increases in women's representation will lead to a process of competitive bidding for women's support from which no party can afford to abstain if it hopes to have electoral success.

Pragmatic arguments make a virtue of difference by contending that through women's involvement, politics will become more constructive and less adversarial. This is of course a controversial claim, but it has some basis. Gender difference is associated with different styles of communication and decision-making. Study after study shows that women and men politicians have different attitudes on a range of issues (Lovenduski and Norris 2003). Empirical research demonstrates that in countries where women have a significant political presence, changes in political style, discourse and decision-making are associated with their increased presence of women (Duerst-Lahti and Kelly 1995; Karvonen and Selle 1995; Mateo-Diaz 2002). At a time when public distaste for the adversarial conventions of politics and distrust of politicians are at record highs in many countries, supporters argue that increased women's representation could have an extremely significant beneficial impact on political institutions.

Difference arguments

A third set of arguments is based on concepts of difference. The core argument is that women will bring a different style and approach to politics which will change it for the better, an effect that is of benefit to all. A useful way to explore the implications of gender difference for citizenship is to consider the universal citizen, the disembodied political agent of traditional democratic theory. The interaction of gender relations and social difference has important effects on the political power of different groups of women and men. Both their basis in difference arguments and their effects on the resources of different groups of women and men require us to take full account of the inequalities that are embedded in citizenship.

In her extension of Carol Pateman's arguments in *The Sexual Contract*, Ruth Lister argued that one result of feminist advocacy is that the 'universalised cloak of the abstract, disembodied individual has been cast aside to reveal a definitely male citizen and a white, heterosexual non-disabled one at that' (1997: 66). In other words, its universalism previously disguised the ways in which citizenship was affected by gender and made possible a mistaken belief that men could represent all of women's interests. By contrast, the effects of sex difference are historically clear. For much of history neither women nor men were citizens. When citizenship was reinvented as an idea in the wake of the French Revolution of 1789, it was a blatantly male construction. For example, until the last part of the nineteenth century, married women in Britain and the USA did not exist as independent individuals in terms of the law. This was an effect of the doctrine of coverture, which meant that women lived under the 'cover' of their male head of household who exercised citizenship on behalf of his family. Coverture was changed in both countries by a series of other legal measures – all the product of intensive feminist struggle. Thus, as Ursula Vogel (1988, 1994) has argued, women once stood outside civil society, and were connected to it only through dependence and subordination. This legacy of legal exclusion, now corrected in most countries, had two important lasting consequences. First, women took their place as citizens in institutions and organizations largely arranged for the convenience of men. Second, a widespread sense that women were less competent as citizens than men persisted for most of the twentieth century.

Public and Private Spheres

Ruth Lister argues that the exclusion of women from citizenship is partly a product of essentialist categorizations of men's and women's capacities and qualities. She writes that the actually male, but formally abstract, disembodied individual who was the citizen of political theory and constitutional law for so long existed only because a distinction between public and private life created a divide that women did not cross. In public life, because women were not present, men's concerns and bodies were the unquestioned norm. Relegated to the private sphere, women were the invisible supporters of public life through the provision of care, reproduction and other unpaid work. One consequence of such separation was that it was possible to think about individuals as abstract, disembodied entities because only male bodies were present. Bodies were absent from political discourse and women's bodies were for the most part absent from public life. It was therefore possible to overlook the fact that women's work made public life possible.

A ludicrous set of conventions attended women's absence. Bodies had no place in civil society, where to be present one had to transcend one's embodiment, something men but not women were deemed capable of doing. Women's admission to citizenship was therefore an admission to the public sphere on different terms from men because it meant that account had to be taken of the hitherto invisible necessity of the roles played by women in private life. Women, 'on entering the public sphere . . . [were] . . . not able to shed the sexualised and familialised skin that bound them to the private' (Lister 1997: 70–1). Hence, concludes Lister, the question of women's inclusion is not a simple numerical one, but involves their status as 'other' and their manifestations in unruly bodies and messy relationships, a theme that is a major concern in recent feminist writing.

Political Institutions

Political institutions are the organizations, formal and informal rules, processes and procedures through which politics is done. Political institutions are also gender regimes with distinctive ideologies of how women and men should act, think and feel. They control access to resources and affect the availability of alternatives to their gendered ideologies (Connell 1987). They affect the way in which political representation works in practice. Established institutions have the capacity to preserve traditions and cultures, prevent or slow change and protect elites. Political institutions therefore may be expected to protect and preserve traditional cultures and elites. In Britain such protection operates through an arcane set of practices, many of which have continued for centuries. In Parliament, for example, prior to modernization, legislation was made according to practices devised for the nineteenth century or earlier, when representation was not thought of in terms of democracy at all (Judge 1999). Practices included a fair amount of ritual and fancy dress. The conventions assume that the legislator is male. For example, although what legislators wear probably does not affect their decision-making capacities, they are required to wear a tie when speaking in the Commons. In October 2002, during debates on the modernization of House of Commons working practices, Ken Brennan, MP for Cardiff West, was ordered to leave the Chamber because he attempted to speak without wearing a tie. Reflecting the sexist culture of the House, Michael

Fabricant (Conservative, Lichfield) said that he had noticed that 'for the first time in [his] experience an MP had spoken without a tie', but he failed, as *The Times* commentator noted, either to have noticed the presence of women MPs or perhaps that they were MPs (*The Times*, 29 October 2002). Not only is the legislator of the conventions male, he is also a man of a particular conservative and Victorian type. It could be worse. Until 1998 both men and women were required to wear a top hat when making a point of order.

The top hat and tie requirements are manifestations of the embedded masculinity that characterizes all male institutions. The historic exclusion of women from politics permitted a set of male-centred institutional practices to evolve without comment or protest. The continued relative exclusion of women permits the persistence of such practices. The distinction made between public and private spheres, so important to contemporary democratic thought, also plays a part. The public–private divide separates traditional men's and women's roles into two spheres, relegating women to the private sphere. This separation underpins a set of dichotomies observed by Ruth Lister 'to be saturated with gendered implications and associations, which permeate the very fabric of citizenship' (1997: 69).

The polarization expressed by Lister is a familiar component of feminist theory. The abstract public citizen is male in the sense that he is composed of traditionally masculine roles and characteristics. He is universal, rational and capable of impartiality. He is concerned with the public interest, able to display and apply abstract standards of justice. Independent, reactive, heroic and strong, he will uphold the realms of freedom and the human (Lister 1997: 69). As Lister writes:

> [He] stands and acts in the public sphere as the representative of the household which he leads through the hierarchical institution of marriage, the locus of male citizen's power over female non citizens. *At different times in history* he can be seen as the citizen owner of property or labour and as the citizen

27

soldier. . . . The warrior hero has left a particularly marked imprint on . . . citizenship . . . against which women were measured as weak and incapable. (1997: 70; my emphasis)

In contrast the 'private', female non-citizen is 'particular, embodied and rooted in nature'. Her concerns are private, partial and domestic. She is emotional, irrational and weak. Her interests, such as they are, are in maintaining the 'realm of necessity' in the domestic sphere (Lister 1997: 70–1).

The work of Lister and others shows how, historically, women's bodies and their association with the body and nature has disqualified them from citizenship. The argument about embodiment and citizenship works similarly for political representation. Members and observers of all male organizations, assemblies, workplaces and teams can ignore the effects of gender, thus disguising the masculine nature of the institutions by treating it as universal. But when women are present the disguise is exposed and practices and procedures are disrupted. Small ceremonies and rituals are exposed as childish (boyish) and silly. Even so, the institutions play a major part in the construction of identity, and hence themselves help to create gender characteristics, a point to which I return below.

The Political Dimensions of Feminist Ideas

Feminism

Like politics, feminism is not a single, easily expressed idea. The word is used to encapsulate a variety of positions and interests and means different things to different groups, so much so that it has become commonplace to speak of 'feminisms' rather than of a singular feminism. Thus instead of offering a definition, it is more useful to describe the common characteristics of discussions of feminism. Most definitions of feminisms attribute to them a concern with women's inferior position in society and with the discrimination women encounter because of their sex (Delmar 1986; Freedman 2001; Oakley and Mitchell 1997). Beyond that baseline, agreement collapses. Historically, a concern with women's issues predates the use of the term 'feminist' and claims by some women to feminism are disputed (Delmar 1986). Moreover, in contemporary political life it is common for women's advocates to avoid the use of the term 'feminist' because it has been stigmatized and is thought to be electorally or otherwise politically disadvantageous. This is similar to the 'I am not a feminist but . . .' syndrome, in which women's advocates do not or will not recognize their position as feminist.

Arguably, willingness to call oneself a feminist is part of being one. Feminists who assert that it is important to separate feminists from other women's advocates (Delmar 1986) further complicate definition. Delmar's argument is important and was influential at the time that she made it. It was a tough test of feminism. The extent of their willingness to declare their feminism is a difference among women politicians that may reflect different circumstances and opportunities. Not all women politicians are feminists and not all of those who are, are willing to say so. However, whether and when and how feminist politicians 'come out' is a matter for empirical research. If that research is to be possible, then we cannot insist on self-identification as a criterion of feminism. All we can do is ensure that the different ways of justifying claims made on behalf of women are made clear and kept distinct.

Equality and difference

A central feminist preoccupation that affects the arguments in this book is the distinction between claims made on the basis of equality and those made on the basis of difference. Equality-based claims stress women's entitlements to be in politics on the same terms and in the same numbers as men.

Difference-based claims (sometimes termed 'maternal' or 'social' feminism) imply that women have particular characteristics or interests that entitle them to representation. Both the equality and the difference cases for equal representation have many variations.

The distinctions are less clear in matters of political representation than in other areas of women's advocacy. This is because arrangements for political representation evolved through compromises and agreements in which ideas and entitlements overlapped and original definitions were obscured. The different implications of the two bases of feminism are sometimes thought to be stark. For many critics, the equality position suggests that women's claims for political representation will, if successful, turn them into political men. By contrast, the difference position implies that, in sufficient numbers, the presence of women representatives will change the practice and nature of politics.

On the one hand, in keeping with difference arguments, feminists contest the division between public and private life that, in theory at least, is the boundary between politics and other activities. On the other hand, in keeping with the logic of equality, feminists argue that women are entitled to their place in the world of formal politics, however it is constructed. According to the first argument, the political representation of women necessitates the collapse of public–private divisions and, presumably, a resulting institutional transformation. According to the second argument, claims for women's representation are satisfied by the admission of sufficient women into already existing institutions. The strategy problem is obvious. Presence, which involves the acceptance of the existing rules of the game, is required if the new rules are to be made. Equality is needed if difference is to be compensated and difference must be recognized if equality is to be achieved.

Throughout the history of feminism there have been tensions between proponents of the two strands. A considerable amount of scholarship has explored and theorized the contrasts, connections and overlaps of the two positions. Running through much of that scholarship is a fear that emphasis on one or other basis of feminism will undermine the important insights and claims supported by the other. Hence feminists who make claims from equality principles are charged with interest only in the quantitative dimensions of political representation, whilst difference feminists are criticized for ignoring the role of politics and the state.

In practice and in scholarship most feminists are well aware of the problems and promises of both positions, and most attempt to keep elements of both equality and difference arguments in play when making claims or discussing movement theories and practices. Anyone reading the current corpus of work on gender and politics soon becomes aware that the equality/difference tension is an extremely useful scholarly convention that helps to organize discussions of movement theory and practice. The disadvantage of the convention is that disagreements get exaggerated, silences are overinterpreted and boundaries are overdrawn.

Such polarization may make a good forcing ground for theory, but in the practice of politics, both broadly and narrowly defined, boundaries frequently collapse. In the process, both difference and equality considerations are included and illuminated but also distorted. For example, women politicians seeking election to an ancient legislature may claim equality on the basis of fairness, a claim that legitimizes their entry on the basis of special measures of some kind. In the course of debate, it will be argued that only women can represent women, a claim that admits difference considerations and raises expectations about the kind of representation that will then be available. Observers and commentators may then criticize the women for being less knowledgeable and effective than the men who preceded and accompanied them, at the same time as criticizing them for not altering the composition, practices and procedures of legislative politics. All of this happened in response to the 1997 election of 120 women to the House of Commons. Both claimants and their opponents drew on equality and difference arguments, largely to suit the particular context. The point I am trying to make is that both bases for claiming representation are necessary and flawed. Both equality and difference arguments support and undermine feminists and their opponents who also draw on arguments about democracy and representation to frame their writing and advance their claim – or whatever the project may be.

Claiming the right of representation is an iterative process in which the particular context will greatly affect the way supporters proceed. The history of feminism shows that women's claims fare best when feminist movements are united. Possibilities for such unity are undermined by gender difference. But the conditions for unity are also greatly affected by the political system in which they take place. Demographic, institutional and cultural factors influence movement possibilities. These influences are well illustrated by the experiences of nineteenth- and early twentieth-century feminism.

The history of feminist mobilization is often understood to be built around the issue of suffrage, and the many other accomplishments and preoccupations of the first wave of the movement are thus sometimes obscured. The suffrage struggles were interesting and important and their concerns are central to the concerns of this book. Suffrage movements took place alongside other feminist campaigns in movements that claimed both substantive and descriptive representation. Many of the issues that interest us today were around, and a matter of discussion and struggle, when feminists first organized. It was as part of a diverse and radical set of campaigns that the struggle for women's political citizenship began.

Feminist Movements

Nineteenth-century feminists understood, if sometimes implicitly, that it was necessary to politicize 'private' life. They understood that women's disadvantaged private roles contributed greatly to their unequal public status. Interest in both the public and private sphere was most evident at the places where they came together, where the state legislated about private, that is, family matters. Where the law was silent, campaigns were more difficult. Issues of the body were particularly vexed because there were huge constraints on the understanding and discussion of the body and of sexuality in Victorian England. The rise of feminism in the late nineteenth century coincided with an era in which sexuality and morality were elided. Victorian society was greatly concerned with and fearful about sexual matters, which became subject to increasing control and manipulation. By the end of the century there was legislation on the statute books about many 'private' areas of what was now deemed to be morality. Laws governed the sexual preferences of individuals, marital relations, marriage, divorce, venereal disease, prostitution, male homosexuality and incest. The state regulation of sexuality coincided with the growth of separate spheres of male and female life.

Victorian perceptions of sexuality, which we may extrapolate from a vast literature, including medical texts, religious tracts and the output of a thriving pornography industry, were based upon a fundamental belief in the notion of sexual difference. According to this belief, men and women were what they were because of biology. Biological differences between the sexes were therefore the central determinant of their separate social roles.

The nineteenth-century characterization of 'separate spheres' was an ideological change. That is, the way women were regarded changed, but not necessarily what women did. In earlier times women had been seen as the lustful sex whose tempting, seducing sexuality was responsible for man's downfall. The biblical tale of Eve was only one myth in a number of similar belief systems. But the nineteenth-century English keynote was the passivity and the reluctant nature of women's sexuality (respectable women, anyway). The apparent belief in women's passivity appears in retrospect to have been part of an apparatus of control. There was a sexual basis to women's separate social sphere. The bodies of women needed to be controlled and regulated. Part of the strategy of control was to establish the inferior nature of women's bodies. For example, parallels were drawn between men's sexual and political powers. Medical men warned that higher education would endanger women's reproductive capacities. Economic change was also supported and affected by this ideology.

Home and workplace became increasingly separated with the rise of industrial capitalism. The workplace was in the 'public' world and came to be regarded as brutal, dirty and immoral in a new sexual sense. Women needed to be protected, it was felt, from the moral contamination that participating in public (that is, male) workplaces would involve. Women's world was the home in 'separate spheres' ideology, and it was also women who had the task of protecting 'morality'. One by-product was that women were designated the morally superior sex. An implication was that it was important for feminist campaigners to have impeccable personal reputations.

'Separate spheres' morality sanctioned a double standard that feminists of course attacked. They campaigned against the double standard itself, notably in the campaigns against the Contagious Diseases Acts. Feminists also campaigned against the legal manifestations of dependence and the double standard, especially the inequalities relating to marriage, most importantly the Married Women's Property Act. There are many contemporary resonances. For example, marital violence was an important issue. Legal opinion did little to inhibit male violence within marriage, as jurists held that husbands were entitled to give wives moderate correction. And women were frightened to use what protection the law afforded them from immoderate correction. Thus, an article by Frances Power Cobbe (a prominent nineteenth-century British feminist campaigner and writer on the issue of domestic violence against women) about marital violence in the 1870s reports the ghastly tale of a woman who appeared before a magistrate without a nose. She maintained that she had bitten it off herself rather than implicate her husband.

Feminists believed that marital violence – wife abuse as it was called – was a product of alcohol abuse. Feminist and temperance movements tended to overlap and there were many feminist calls on women not to marry men who had not signed the pledge. Marriage itself was an important issue for Victorian feminists. Inequality was seen to stem from 'coverture' and the issue of property. The acquisition of citizenship brought entitlement to own property and made autonomy possible. Increasingly the campaigns for substantive reforms led feminists to claim political representation.

The campaign for the women's vote in Britain was protracted, sometimes violent and highly political. It politicized much else in the course of its history. The first women's suffrage committee in Britain met in 1866. The suffrage advocates at first assumed an early victory because they believed the rhetoric of those politicians who advocated equality and saw the argument for the inclusion of women as self-evident.

The movement for suffrage connected with ideas that became increasingly influential. From the distance of the twenty-first century, it is possible to argue that nineteenth-century feminism was largely difference-based. Although some socialists argued that important differences between women and men were socially determined, few campaigners were prepared to abandon arguments based on motherhood. Whilst equality and difference arguments were made in sometimes fierce debates among feminists, in the nineteenth century many agreed that women should be in the home. However, home, as Paula Baker notes in relation to the USA movement, was a basis for political action. It was a place where women 'combined political activity, domesticity and republican thought through motherhood. Although outside of formal politics, mothering was crucial: by raising virtuous sons, they insured the survival of the republic' (1984: 624). Baker shows how US feminists drew on republican political theory to claim that the domestic sphere was a basis for political rights. British feminists made similar claims. Millicent Fawcett and Emily Pfeiffer believed that women needed political influence because they were mothers. They argued that, as mothers, women needed to be able, by the exercise of their vote, to force legislators to consider the domestic as well as the public sphere (Lewis 1987: 9).

On the basis of motherhood, therefore, some feminists made arguments for access to formal education and involvement in public affairs. They used the canons of domesticity to claim rights. The claims were sometimes essentialist. They frequently contained an assumption of women's moral superiority, an assumption that became a major but double-sided argument in claims for political rights. Some feminists argued for separate spheres of influence to ensure their moral superiority was felt, while others argued that women's superiority entitled them to be admitted to public life on an equal basis. There was a belief, even among liberal feminists, that the maternal role of women led men and women to possess different values.

Maternalism was invoked as a force for justice in the world, but motherhood was a condition that constrained woman's opportunities and limited their power because it, or the potential of it, was the basis of dependency. Based on difference, maternalist arguments for equality contained contradictory strands that were put to good use by opponents of feminism. These arguments are well described elsewhere (Freedman 2001; Kaplan 1992; Squires 1999). I sketch them here to illustrate my contention that in practical terms much of the nineteenth-century feminist claim for political equality was also based on difference.

By the beginning of the twentieth century women could vote and stand for office in local elections in a number of countries, including the USA and Britain. New Zealand had already enfranchised women, as had some US states. In the first decades of the twentieth century a wave of national enfranchisement of women took place, some of which was revoked when democracies collapsed in the 1930s. At the end of the Second World War another wave of voting rights for women took place, and by 2004 only Kuwait and the United Arab Emirates (where the legislature is appointed) denied women the right to vote.

Women won voting rights as part of wider changes in political systems. For example, in Britain and the USA suffrage debates occurred at a time when the functions of government were changing as various parts of the state were increasing their social welfare and economic roles. Changes in state roles and functions and the expansion of government into social regulation and protection made it possible for women to build public power from their domestic situation (Baker 1984). Politics became more concerned with issues that were 'appropriate' for women. At the same time, male public roles were changing, partly, of course, influenced by the campaigns of feminists (Freeman 2000). Thus women first won the vote at a time when the meaning of the vote was changing. The extension of the franchise itself reduced the value of each vote, while the enlarged electorate did not alter the male dominance of governing institutions.

In neither Britain nor the USA did suffrage usher in a new era of women's politics. The women who campaigned for the vote, and were a large pool of the potential candidates afterwards, did not find their way into national politics. The underlying reason was gender difference. Women were divided. They voted according to their family, class, religious and regional interests and did not prioritize their sex. At first, politicians feared that women would vote as a block. Political parties feared and took precautions against the possible foundation of women's parties by making explicit appeals for women's votes. Male legislators enacted policies designed to appeal to women. In Britain, for example, the first post-suffrage Parliament passed legislation to improve rights in marriage and divorce, to regulate provision for maternity care and to secure payments from fathers to support their children. In the USA the Sheppard Towner Act of 1921 made provision for maternal care and the introduction of prohibition was widely, if incorrectly, seen as a victory for feminist reformers.

These points are necessarily speculative. Prior to the widespread use of surveys, voting patterns were not so closely analysed as they are today. So far as anyone could tell, however, women, although they were thought to be and probably were frequently more likely than men to vote for parties of the centre right, did not vote as a block. Party politicians soon found they had no need to think of women as a separate electoral constituency.

Feminism and Party Politics

From the time of the early suffrage campaigns, party divisions inhibited feminist unity. Pugh (1992: 70) notes how Labour Party women's groups did not join feminist umbrella organizations, preferring to make their own Labour-only groups. Labour, Liberal and Conservative parties established women's sections and allowed women to become members after 1918, but the sections were not in the party mainstream and aspirant women politicians had to win mainstream support if they were to succeed. Parties attempted to manage women's constituencies while continuing to support a male-dominated mainstream. In the Labour Party, for example, although there were reserved places for women on the ruling National Executive Committee, these were filled by the block votes of the male-dominated affiliated trade unions rather than by the votes of members of the women's sections. Thus men, not women, decided who the women representatives were to be.

In the Conservative Party, special arrangements were made for women members. Measures included separately organized and employed (and lower paid) women's agents and places were reserved for women in the party hierarchy. Neither party offered the opportunity for women members to choose their own representatives on internal bodies. The first women MPs were chosen by party selectors in systems dominated by men. Although there were differences among women within the parties, Labour and Conservative parties defined women's public roles and interests in distinctive ways. Labour women emphasized class interests, while Conservative women took responsibility for family and moral (meaning sexual) matters. Inevitably, these emphases offered different visions of women's interests.

To accommodate their women voters and supporters, political parties incorporated difference arguments into their rhetoric, stressing the roles of mothers. Bea Campbell (1987) has described the way that Tory women took womanly matters into the heart of politics in a highly sexualized discourse that, amongst other things, reflected a belief that crime was the result of the disruption of sex roles. Conservative women believed in marriage, but also that wives had rights.

As the public face of the feminist movement declined, the organized women's movement continued to be active. Feminist campaigning organizations such as the Townswomen's Guild were founded to advocate women's interests. However, public loyalties were often to one or other political party. The costs of affiliation were high. The Co-operative Women's Guild, for example, affiliated through the co-operative movement to the Labour Party, found its funding cut when it supported easier divorce laws on feminist grounds and antagonized the Catholic members of the co-operative movement (Black 1989).

Such problems remind us how important autonomous feminist movements are to the success of women's claims. Then, as now, an autonomous women's movement was necessary to ensure advocacy of women's interests. Jo Freeman shows how, in the United States, party women were sidelined and marginalized by Democratic and Republican parties for most of the twentieth century, even though both parties attracted women activists (Freeman 2000). Her findings are reflected in studies of parties in Britain and other European democracies (Graves 1994; Lovenduski and Norris 1993; Maguire 1998).

The marginalization of women's sections meant that women wishing to pursue a political career had to operate in the party mainstream to acquire the power base necessary for political careers. So high were the barriers that few women made it over them, and those who did were under pressure to behave like political men, to deny they were feminists and to operate the traditional barriers to women. Numerous examples of token women pulling ladders up after them are reported in early accounts of women's representation. For example, Pugh reports how Margaret Bondfield's rise via the trade unions to Parliament and cabinet in the 1920s was accompanied by a decline in the status of women 'behind her' (1992: 99–100).

Party pressures for conformity were not always effective. Threaded through the histories, biographies and other accounts are numerous indications that early women MPs were not party loyalists to the exclusion of all women's concerns. For example, although Nancy Astor was never active in the feminist movement, she felt a responsibility to act for women. She raised issues of sex equality and difference in the House of Commons (Fox 1998). Sixty years later, the avowedly anti-feminist Margaret Thatcher paid close attention to improving women's access to public appointments and consistently increased the budget of the Equal Opportunities Commission throughout her years of office (Bashevkin 1998). It seems that, even under quite difficult and constraining conditions, women representatives sometimes acted for women.

In Britain, the 1920s were years of major social reform in which significant parts of the agenda of nineteenth-century feminism were enacted. These achievements owed much to a few women MPs and to the efforts of independent women's movements outside Parliament. The women's movement ebbed and flowed in the course of the twentieth century. Sometimes dispersed, sometimes largely elite-maintained, campaigns, lobbies or debates driven by feminists were continuously in evidence. The numerous areas of feminist concerns often generated some explicitly political activities and frequently provoked an anti-feminist response. However, women's advocates, including women MPs from all political parties, continued to press for sex equality measures. They were supported by women organized at party grass roots, in trade unions and other professional organizations (Lovenduski 1986; Meehan 1985).

The Women's Liberation Movement

A strong autonomous feminist movement reappeared at the end of the 1960s. Generational difference became a leitmotif of the period. Emphasis on 'traditional' domestic life and on the materialist values of the 1950s was increasingly challenged by a privileged generation that was not interested in politics as usual. The story of the emergence of women's liberation from the movements of the 1960s has been well told elsewhere (Coote and Campbell 1987; Freeman 1975; Kaplan 1992). The decade was one of increasing pressure from the feminist movement for women's rights. Not only did the Women's Liberation Movement emerge, with its claims for the emancipation of women, but also the more prosaic and long-standing campaigns gained a new lease of life. Feminist reform campaigns were revitalized as equal pay claims and movements for changes in laws to liberalize divorce, to decriminalize abortion provision and to provide for equal opportunities mobilized (Lovenduski 1986).

The 1970s began with widespread expectations of continuing social change, signalled by the passage of new legislation for sex equality in Britain and Western Europe. In the Nordic states, where women were already comparatively better represented in legislatures than elsewhere, women organized for equality of representation, but their early success was an exception. Elsewhere, despite far-reaching changes in women's lives in terms of access to education, contraception, divorce and paid work, there was little change in women's political representation. Britain, the USA and France were amongst the worst offenders. The strong movements for women's liberation did not prioritize issues of political representation, preferring the freedom of social movement activity.

Over the course of the 1970s much of the promise of the Women's Liberation Movement faded as the feminist movement became increasingly fragmented and activists became preoccupied with the peace and environmental movements. Such preoccupations continued through the 1980s. However, there was an afterglow. Concerns of the body were effectively politicized, issues of sexuality stayed on the political agenda, the women's studies movement emerged and claims for sex equality became more insistent.

By the end of the 1970s, confidence in the success of the movement began to falter. Demands were narrowed and more pragmatic politics were pursued as growing resistance to extensions to rights already granted made the dreams of transforming society seem unrealizable. The Women's Liberation Movement in Britain did not prioritize campaigns for equality of political representation. By the time it stopped holding national meetings in 1978 it had agreed to seven demands, none of which explicitly included equal political representation.[1]

When the issue was taken up, advocates encountered great resistance. Movements to gain equality faltered in political institutions in both Britain and the United States. American equal rights feminists were successful in getting the Equal Rights Amendment (ERA) to the Constitution through Congress, after which it went to the states for ratification. Thirty-eight states needed to ratify the amendment by 1982. In the event, only thirty-five states did so. Its failure was the

---

1 (1) Equal pay, equal education and opportunity; (2) 24-hour nurseries; (3) free contraception; (4) abortion on demand (agreed in 1970; by 1975 picked up); (5) financial and legal independence for women; (6) an end to all discrimination against lesbianism and a woman's right to choose her own sexuality; (7) freedom from violence and sexual coercion.

result of backlash. In the early 1970s a coordinated right-wing anti-feminist coalition emerged in the USA to oppose not only the ERA, but also the liberalized abortion and benefit regimes.

Feminist priorities in Britain appeared to change after 1979 when Margaret Thatcher became Britain's first woman prime minister, introducing an era in which arguments for women's political representation became more interesting to feminist activists. Feminist concern was partly a matter of defending the interests of many women, as unemployment rose, benefit availability declined and it became clear to a new generation of feminists that public politics mattered. In Britain, a reconfiguration of political competition appeared to offer new possibilities for women's representation. At the beginning of the 1980s the political structure seemed to be changing, and the changes had implications for feminizing politics. The short-lived new Social Democratic Party raised the issue of women's representation, as did the growing Green Party. Labour and Liberal Party women mobilized around representation issues. From that time, albeit with some ebbs and flows, the issue of women's presence in politics was on the British political agenda. Gender politics in the USA polarized on party lines as feminists became part of the new Democratic Party coalition and anti-feminists aligned with the Republican Party.

As the Women's Liberation Movement ebbed, it left in its wake revitalized and repoliticized groups able to consolidate around an agreed set of women's issues. In the ensuing years, feminists continued to campaign against violence to women, for abortion provision and for equal pay and opportunity. In each campaign there were divisions as positions polarized on predictable equality and difference positions.

By this time, recognition of the importance of securing political representation was widespread, if not universally agreed in the movements. Thus, the last part of the twentieth century saw new movements for the political representation of women. These demanded that governments should require the inclusion of women in institutions of representation. Feminists organized campaigns for compulsory quotas of women in legislatures, assemblies and appointed committees and commissions. They mobilized demands for reserved seats in legislatures and for parity, defined as the equal representation of women and men. They also intervened in movements for constitutional and institutional reforms in order to insert provision for women's presence into decisions about reform. The story of their successes and failures is one of a long learning process in which setbacks and defeats led to renewed campaigns, redefinitions of issues and, eventually, growing success at claiming political equality.

3

Obstacles to Feminizing Politics

The correction of women's political underrepresentation is work in progress, much of which remains to be done. By 2003 only 39 nation-states had ever selected a woman as prime minister or president. Worldwide, fewer than 10 per cent of cabinet ministers, 20 per cent of lower ranking government ministers and 15 per cent of legislators were women (IPU). These low figures are historic highs, achieved after decades of struggle.

Although there is significant regional variation, the underrepresentation of women is a persistent political fact of life in modern states, present across all types of institutional arrangements and cultures. It is one of the few generalizations that it is safe to make about the position of women.

How can such underrepresentation be explained? The explanations are complex; the absence of women from representative offices is the result of a combination of institutional and social factors. The social obstacles are the most familiar. Women experience three main social obstacles to becoming politicians. First, they have fewer of the resources needed to enter politics. Women are poorer than men and are less likely to be employed in occupations that are supportive of political activism. Second, various lifestyle constraints mean women have less time for politics. Family and other caring responsibilities are typically undertaken by women, reducing their time for other activities. Third, the job of politics is coded as male, which inhibits women from seeking political careers and also impedes the recruitment of those who come forward.

Constitutional and legal obstacles have also been important. Democratic states have laws that determine who electors and representatives may be and how representation takes place. Rules about representatives may specify the characteristics that a representative should have. Age, citizenship and residency are frequently specified. Women were barred by law from being representatives in many states until recently. By 2003 only some Middle Eastern states continued with such exclusion. These were Kuwait, Qatar, Saudi Arabia, Oman and the United Arab Emirates. More generally, the type of electoral law a system operates affects its representativeness in various ways and is thought to have an effect on opportunities for women to be elected as representatives. In general, more women are elected under party list proportional representation (PR) systems than under majoritarian electoral systems, although there is considerable variation within each type of system (Norris 2004).

Although most of the possible explanations turn out to be widespread phenomena, few are universal. Women's political disadvantages are embedded in particular social and institutional arrangements, subject to many different constraints. In this chapter I explore barriers to women's political representation in modern democracies. I use the example of the Westminster system to illustrate my arguments. I examine in detail the barriers to women's presence in the House of Commons and the barriers to their political recruitment in British political parties. I argue that British political institutions are characterized by a culture of traditional masculinity that is a major obstacle to women. I describe the culture and draw on feminist social theory to explain the processes through which it developed. This culture supports institutional sexism in the political system. Although there are some signs of recent change, there is considerable evidence of persisting institutional sexism in the political parties and in the House of Commons.

Sexism is not the only barrier to women's presence at Westminster, where it is comparatively difficult for any recently mobilized groups to gain a foothold. In constitutional terms the UK has a high threshold of representation compared to other representative democracies. The Westminster electoral system is based on single-member constituencies in which the winning candidate needs to secure only a simple majority of the vote, a system known to be associated with low levels of women's representation. Westminster is no longer the only significant site of British political representation. A process of constitutional change has brought new assemblies into being in Scotland, Wales and Northern Ireland. These assemblies are elected on PR systems which, in Scotland and Wales, have facilitated measures to increase the inclusion of women. In Northern Ireland, advocates of women's representation have been less successful, though some progress has been made. The UK system therefore provides a good illustrative example of the impact of various electoral systems on women's representation (see chapter 4).

Institutional Constraints

The laws that regulate political recruitment are only part of the process, which is also affected by the various institutions to which and through which recruitment takes place. The institutions that affect the level and nature of women's representation include political parties, elected assemblies and various pressure groups and social movements, including feminist movements. As we have seen, feminists have often been ambivalent about claiming political representation. Part of the reason for that ambivalence is an appreciation that political institutions are characterized by priorities, cultures and practices that privilege certain kinds of masculinity. Feminist engagement with politics takes place in an already well-established set of institutions and practices. Its effectiveness is conditioned by traditional political practices, including voting, participation in parties and associational life, and by attitudes, beliefs and values that are produced and reproduced in particular settings.

When women began to participate in such settings, even if they were not feminist, they affected how they worked. They were, in the words of Nirmal Puwar, 'space invaders' who challenged gender norms by their very presence. The institutions and practices apparently adjusted to and absorbed the invaders with little or no relaxation of their sexism. Hence feminists are concerned that the practice of political representation will require women to behave like the men they seek to replace (Puwar 2004: 65). Joan Acker (1992), for example, refers to the occasional biological female who acts like a social man when she writes about women who were in powerful positions prior to the 1990s.

In practice, then, the most difficult obstacle is the deeply embedded culture of masculinity that pervades political institutions. When women become members of a legislature or other representative assembly, they are normally entering a male domain. For a long time Westminster was one of those places where men gathered with other men. Its ways were the ways of the gentlemen's clubs and public schools that were so important in establishing the norms of appropriate male behaviour. Parliament is masculine. I mean this in the sense that it institutionalizes the norms of the men who founded it and for so many years inhabited it as a wholly male institution. This is why Westminster for so long boasted a rifle range but not a crèche. No conspiracy was necessary to exclude women; indeed, often the exclusion of women was not even a consideration. Like many institutions of the state, the Westminster culture embodies practices that reward traditional forms of masculinity and disallow traditional forms of femininity.

But it is too simple to state that women in such environments become men. The presence of even one woman in a previously all male arena illuminates its gendered nature and exposes its masculine characteristics. The disruptive effects of the entry of women into this environment are well illustrated by the career of Nancy Astor, the first woman to take her seat in the House of Commons. She experienced enormous resistance to her presence. Her most recent biographer writes of the almost overwhelming effort of courage and will needed to stand up to the hostility – petty, persistent and often vicious – from her colleagues in the House of Commons. The hostility came mostly from her own party. There was an unwritten consensus among the Conservatives, her party, that a female MP was by nature wrong. The idea was to freeze her out, cause the maximum embarrassment and humiliation, and so discourage constituencies from adopting other women candidates. Conservatives that she knew well turned away from her, including her two brothers-in-law. They refused to give her a seat at the corner of the bench, forcing her to climb over men's legs. At first they pretended they could not find a lavatory for her and made her walk to the far end of the building. Before a debate on venereal disease, they put the most graphic photographs they could find in the lobby, hoping to embarrass her. They made speeches that they considered unsuitable for a woman's ears. 'Shortly before she died she told her son David that if . . . "I had known how much men would hate it, I would never have dared do it"' (Fox 1998).

When Liberal MP Margaret Wintringham became the second woman to take a seat in the House, she found the feeling of hatred she experienced when she went into the House to be so great that if Nancy Astor was not present in the chamber at the same time, the atmosphere was so unbearable that she had to leave (Fox 1998).

Such resistance is evidence that women representatives, by their very presence, threaten established patterns of behaviour. The institutional masculinity encountered by Astor was of a traditional kind. Historically it was bolstered by a variety of all-male organizations such as public schools, professions and the gentlemen's clubs. In the UK the House of Commons reflects the masculinity of its heyday in the Victorian era.

Why Does the Culture of Traditional Masculinity Persist?

Both gender theory and institutional theory suggest that institutions have considerable capacity to reproduce their cultures. Institutions are able to create and recreate gendered patterns through constantly repeated processes of exclusion. Gender inequalities, whereby some types of masculine behaviour are favoured, are produced and reproduced in political organizations such as legislatures. The underrepresentation of women and their near exclusion from powerful positions is underpinned by a set of practices, discourses and images that are associated with political institutions. For example, in politics leadership is often discussed in terms of military discourses in which war, battle, strength and victory are invoked. Such symbols and images express and reinforce gender divisions. They are embedded in the institution in various ways and may persist long after associated behaviour has become unacceptable in the society outside of the institution.

Institutional Masculinity

The argument that public institutions are characterized by an invisible masculinity draws on the same kinds of argument used by Lister (1997) in her account of the masculinity of citizenship discussed in chapter 2. Research on public institutions in the 1980s and 1990s described in detail the way gender is shaped by public as well as private institutions (Bologh 1990; Davies 1994; Hearn 1989; Jones 1993;

Savage and Witz 1992). The research shows how the shaping of gender by public institutions privileges certain kinds of masculinity and operates to maintain its dominance during periods of change, implementing a kind of insulation process that is familiar to students of political elites. This phenomenon is well expressed by Celia Davies (1994), who argues that cultural codes of masculinity and femininity shape identity from earliest childhood and are encountered and re-encountered in the 'frozen social relations' of institutions. The cultural codes of gendered behaviour do not match exactly the beliefs and behaviour of 'actually existing women and men' – they are cultural codes, hence they are both complicated and idealized, but able to affect women and men. There are numerous competing masculinities and femininities. In real institutions gender biases are not static because gender is relational, that is masculinity and femininity are understood and can be understood only in relation to each other. When one participant in the relationship changes, so must the other. Moreover, the relation of masculinity to femininity, although dominant, is uneasy.

Theories of bureaucracy are a cornerstone of studies of state institutions. Feminists have shown that influential conceptions of bureaucracy are gendered. For example, they have criticized the influential theories of Max Weber about rational bureaucracy, professionalism, leadership and the institutionalization of authority (Bologh 1990; Ferguson 1984; and Jones 1993). Weber's theory of bureaucracy offers a model of how public administration should work. His model maps almost directly onto Lister's male citizen model. It is an ideal type, the main characteristics of which are hierarchy, routine, accountability, regulation, professionalism and impartiality. Feminist critics often elide Weber's descriptions of ideal bureaucracy with practices in 'actually existing bureaucracies'. Whilst unfair to Weber, this does not invalidate their insights into real institutions. They contend that Weber's professional, his rational bureaucrat and his legitimate ruler are the same idealized *man*.

Weber's ideal man is, of course, a construct of a particular idealized masculinity. For example, his ideal public bureaucrat is a rational, impartial, public-minded individual who wishes to make a difference in the world. Such men engage in autonomous action, each behaving rationally in pursuit of individual interest. Relations to each other are aggressive and competitive in a public world of '*hostile strangers*' in which collective action occurs only where power is exercised, where some men dominate everyone else (Bologh 1990). Other men are controlled through fear and loyalty which is institutionalized into hierarchy. Women and femininity are ignored. For example, the significance of women's paid and unpaid work and the dependence of the performance of the rational bureaucrat on domestic labour is unacknowledged or invisible. Love and protection are illusory. Amongst hostile strangers it is possible to accede to codes of femininity only by withdrawing. In the world of the rational bureaucrat, women remain in the private sphere under the protection of men (Bologh 1990; Davies 1994).

The theories of Max Weber and his feminist critics are more complicated than this brief account suggests. Nevertheless, it is clear that feminist accounts of bureaucracy agree that public organizations have institutionalized the predominance of particular masculinities, thereby empowering and advantaging certain men over all (or almost all) women and some men.

Institutional Sexism

Such theoretical claims may be applied to political institutions to illuminate gender biases in personnel, policy and cultures of political organizations, making visible some of the dynamics of gender and politics within organizations. In the terms of this framework, political institutions are gender-biased. Where bias against women and femininity is entrenched, an organization is institutionally sexist. Institutional sexism is evident when an organization is dominated by one sex in terms of its personnel, outcome and practices.

Institutional sexism may be a precondition of modern politics. The spread of public organizations was predicated on the existence of male power over women (and some men) in private life and private organizations. Political institutions such as governments, legislatures and political parties were part of the process in which men in organizations set rules of the game that ensured that the qualifications most likely to be held by some men were better valued and led more reliably to power and rewards. The historical association of state formation with physical strength, violence and war and the importance of the soldier to the formation of the modern state are instances of such processes. Diplomatic, colonial and military policy in most states is formed around a conception of masculinity that places a premium on toughness and force. An idealized separation of state and society parallels and supports a division of labour in which the contribution of women has been rendered unimportant or invisible. In short, institutional sexism pervades political life.

Feminist critics of British politics agree that its organizations and structures institutionalize the predominance of particular masculinities and in so doing support the dominance of some men. Such biases in part reflect women's political underrepresentation. Biases are most apparent in the levels of women's presence at each level of organizational hierarchies. The more powerful the position in any organizational hierarchy, the more likely it is to be dominated by men.

Does such imbalance affect policy? Probably. There is considerable evidence that policy-makers have been poorly attuned to women's interests and perspectives. Institutional sexism ensures that public policy reflects the needs of one sex more than the other in some way. Such biases are manifested at the agenda-setting, formulation and implementation stages of the policy process. Examples abound. Throughout the world the paid and unpaid work of women is undervalued, but male institutional advantage enables men to resist government policies for employment and pay equality between women and men. The male-dominated criminal justice systems, charged with treatment of the survivors of sexual violence, repeatedly fail to implement good practice, even where good will is present.

Institutional sexism supports gender hierarchies in which some male preferences are conditioned, favoured and rewarded, often long after changing gender relations have removed their original purpose. Jeff Hearn believes that public organizations are crucial supporters of often outdated, traditional conceptions of masculinity. He argues that a narrow range of acceptable (heterosexual) masculinity was established with the development and spread of public organizations. Their development created a power base for certain kinds of men who sustained that power over generations by increasing the quantity of sites upon which male power could operate. To exercise that power men were required to succeed in public bureaucracies, firms and other rule-bound hierarchical establishments (Hearn 1989).

Here is a syndrome that biases organizations, shapes rules, norms, structures and policies and makes it extremely difficult for most women and many men to perceive and pursue their gender interests. An example in Britain is the declamatory, adversarial style of Westminster debate that favours rhetoric, speechifying, posturing and arcane practice in the House of Commons rather than cooperation, consensus-seeking and real discussion of alternatives. Political practices involving demagoguery, ruthlessness and aggression require qualities that are culturally accepted in men but not women. Low turnover ensures that new MPs are quickly conditioned into these practices. As MPs learn and are distracted by these conventions, their lack of real power and ability to ensure government accountability may become secondary to their ability to function in Parliament. Even where turnover is high, however, there is evidence that the system of institutional socialization continues to be effective. An example, detailed further in chapter 6, is the 1997 intake of Labour women who soon found they had to conform to parliamentary rules if they were to be effective. Hence, if it is not possible to show that a political institution is intrinsically male, it can be shown that its arrangements support characteristics associated with certain kinds of masculinity.

In the UK, institutional sexism is apparent both in implicit biases and explicit resistance. In the House of Commons, resistance to women by some men continued throughout the twentieth century, expressed in blatant form by MP John Carlisle who in 1987 told the *Evening Standard*:

> 'Women are natural bitches. They mistrust other women and have a general sense of insecurity about representing their interests. The day's work here at the House of Commons is more naturally tackled by a man. Once you start giving women special privileges and pushing them forward – and it's the same with ethnic minorities – you give them a false sense that they are equal to the task.' (Cited in Abdela 1989: 26)

Resistance does not need to be so explicit, although it is surprising how often it is. In the House of Commons itself Teresa Gorman was shaken by the cruelty of some of the MPs: 'Shortly after I got into the House of Commons, Dennis Skinner would shout across the Chamber to me, "Tell us your age! Where's your birth certificate? Here she comes, Harvey Proctor in drag"' (in Abdela 1989: 23). When Joan Ruddock protested in the House about police strip-searching of women at Greenham Common, Conservative MPs opposite shouted '"*Cor*, we'd like to strip search you too"' (Abdela 1989: 26).

There were many reports of such sexism. For example, in 2001 the *Guardian* carried the story of an unnamed Labour woman MP who objected to the routine shouts of 'melons, melons' when she got up to speak. When she complained to the Speaker of the House Betty Boothroyd, she was told that such experiences came with the territory. Boothroyd's advice was to respond by shouting 'chipolatas, chipolatas' the next time it happened (*Guardian*, 11 January 2001). Commenting on the effects of this atmosphere, Clare Short, MP, remarked: ' "Just the style of the House of Commons makes you very aware you are a woman . . . Even the rituals enforce it. For example, if you make a point of order while a division is on, you have to sit down and put a top hat on" ' (Abdela 1989: 24).

Its origins and habits make the House of Commons a brutal example of the dominance of a culture of traditional masculinity. But elements of institutional sexism are to be found throughout political life. Sometimes this is a matter of ignoring the constraints on women's lives. Fiona Mackay's study of Scottish councillors exposes the delegitimization of women's domestic concerns in local political structures. One of her councillors told her:

> 'They have meetings at 3 o'clock – now why do they start a meeting at three? Now if I say "It's not fair, you do realise that schools come out at this time and if I am in a meeting, how am I to pick up the kids from school?" they're not in the least bit interested. In fact, that's better, because that means I can't go to the meeting, and if I am not there I'm less likely to be a nuisance to them . . . and whenever we have tried to get meetings at night or change times they have said, "Well you knew what you were coming into when you put your name forward, we all have to make sacrifices and it suits us to come at this time . . . so too bad!" ' (2001: 168)

Political Parties

If parliament is the warehouse of traditional masculinity in British politics, political parties are its major distributors. In the UK the responses of political parties are crucial to the outcome of women's claims for representation. This is not unusual. In the systems of party government that characterize so many democratic states, the work of equalizing men's and women's representation must begin in the political parties. However, although most have women members and activists, modern political parties tend to be defined in terms of their relationship to government, traditionally an almost exclusively male activity. According to a recent definition, a political party is 'an institution that (a) seeks influence in a state, often by attempting to occupy positions in government, and (b) usually consists of more than a single interest in the society and so to some degree attempts to aggregate interests' (Ware 1996: 5). Parties vary greatly in their organization, ideology, size, policies and the extent of their political significance. Some states are built around a single party (China), others feature parties that are active only at election times (Canada) and others are governed by coalitions of numerous parties (Switzerland, Italy).

Parties are crucial gatekeepers to government office, one of the main channels of political mobilization in a society and a major source of public policy. Although voters choose candidates, they do so only after political parties have limited the options. Electoral systems are matters for government, but candidate selection rules are made inside political parties. Voters express party preferences; hence much of the explanation of the male-dominated profiles of representatives that are so characteristic of modern electoral politics is the result of internal party decisions. It is parties, not voters, that determine the composition of elected assemblies. Moreover, parties often determine who is awarded appointed offices of various kinds, not only at cabinet level but also in state committees and organizations, including women's organizations. For example, in both Chile and France it is party standing, not women's movement experience, that is decisive in determining which women are appointed to the 'state feminist' bodies (Jenson 1990).

The practices and conventions of Parliament are shaped in political parties, where recruitment practices tend to seek to reproduce parliamentary stereotypes. Recent research on women in the British political parties shows them to be institutionally sexist in the sense that they favour certain kinds of masculine behaviour, offer a vision of the world that implicitly accepts the gendered division of labour and resist claims made by women for political power and responsibility. This set of preferences is built into the organizations, rules and procedures of the parties, so that it survives for generation after generation.

The feminization of political parties is therefore important to the representation of women, whether considered in terms of presence in legislatures and governments or in terms of interests and perspectives. However, for much of their history, political parties have been effective barriers to women's presence in elected office, a pattern well described by Barbara Nelson and Najma Chowdhury (1994). Drawing on evidence from forty-three countries, they reported that women were more likely to get power when political parties were dormant or in disarray during some major regime event. When parties were re-established, women lost ground. Such evidence may tell us why women are typically less likely than men to be members of political parties and why so many women prefer informal and often less effective ad hoc political activity.

Parties vary in their hospitality to women both within and across systems. British political parties are frequently criticized for their excessive 'masculinity'. What is meant here is not so much that they are male organizations, although at leadership levels they generally have been. The argument that the parties are 'masculine' points out how in their different ways the parties have been built around unacknowledged traditional conceptions of gender relations. The argument is analagous to the one made above about traditional legislatures. Thus, although since obtaining the vote women could be members of political parties and their role was often important, they were subordinate. For decades men's and women's roles in parties were ordered by traditional conceptions of masculinity and femininity. The practices were largely accepted, though there were always some resistors among women members.

Party Ideologies

Political parties institutionalize ideas about politics that have gendered implications. Party ideologies are the basis of their enduring reputations and, according to many accounts, fundamental to voter and member trust. Parties may change their ideologies, but only slowly and in tune with wider social change. As institutions, they are able to carry ideals forward from one generation to the next. To paraphrase Putnam (1993), institutions are able both to shape political outcomes and to carry attitudes and behaviour into the future because they shape and are shaped by the identities of the men and women who constitute them. That the institutional sexism of the parties is apparently invisible to mainstream analysts of their ideologies and organizations is a major failing. The vast political science of party politics pays little attention to the effects of gender. Yet gender effects are present in various ways in party life and are reflected in both their ideologies and structures. Moreover, recently, major changes in gender relations have begun to impact on political parties. Thus any study of political parties that fails to take account of gender effects will be inadequate.

How then may we determine if a political party is institutionally sexist? First, it is necessary to outline the standard accounts of party culture, then to consider, as best we can, its gendered dimensions in terms of their susceptibility to feminist arguments for equality, using the categories of justice, pragmatic and difference arguments outlined in chapter 2. In his characterization of the ideologies of the major UK parties, Paul Webb describes the Conservative Party ideology as more a matter of 'dispositions' to protect the established social, political and economic order, this to be done by securing and retaining political power. The Conservatives' 'set of dispositions' includes the rejection of ideas of abstract rights and the effectiveness of social engineering, a belief that the very longevity of traditions is evidence of their utility, a belief in common sense – defined as what usually happens – hierarchy, leadership and authority in an organic society that should be able to maintain its balance by being allowed to evolve rather than be reformed. Social reform is justified only when necessary to appease the masses and promote social unity (Webb 2000: 90–2). Within this almost seamless set of ideas there are divisions and differences that feed occasional divisions in the party. There is a persisting faultline between those who emphasize tradition, community and evolution and those who favour individualism, enterprise and markets.

There is little in the Conservatives' 'set of dispositions' to comfort feminists, and almost nothing to suggest policies of political recruitment that will prioritize the equality of women and men MPs. However, this party has until recently received majority support from women voters. Moreover, for many years its organizational rules reserved places for women at all levels of the party hierarchy (Maguire 1998). Organizationally, however, the party members had no means of controlling its leadership as parliamentary wings, central office and branches were separate until the Hague reforms of 1997. In the Conservative Party, only pragmatic arguments for women's representation are likely to have much purchase. Party ideology offers no ideals of egalitarianism or popular participation on which women's advocates could draw to claim equality of representation. The main resource for supporters of women's equality is the party commitment to power. The historic but now fading dependence on women's votes, the need to win elections and, for many younger Conservatives, to modernize the party offer possibilities to make pragmatic arguments for sex equality. However, despite growing pressure from women activists, the Conservatives continue to resist taking special measures to ensure the nomination of women as candidates for safe seats.

The Labour Party, by contrast, has an egalitarian tradition. However, sex equality has not been a party priority. Historically Labour has sought social equality, defined in terms of class. Internal divisions have turned around whether equality is best promoted by fostering growth (not always possible) or by redistribution policies. These arguments were cross-cut by a common prioritization of class differences. Thus the ideology of the party expressed in its discourse, rhetoric and policies was founded on principles of class equality. Class-based ideology has always been the basis of internal divisions underpinning a constant factionalism in the party. Generally, the divisions were controlled by a dominant alliance of pragmatic parliamentarians and key trade-unionists skilled at operating the party's complex federal structure and system of representation. Claims for other equalities by groups based on gender, race or physical ability were, if regarded at all, secondary to class.

The place of women in this canon was well illustrated by the way they were members of the party. From 1918 women members were integrated through women's sections that had no guaranteed say in decision-making and were cut off from the main party organization. Although five places for women were reserved on the ruling National Executive Committee (NEC), these were filled by trade unions which selected women whose first priority was their unions' interest, whether or not that interest coincided with the views of party women. Until the 1990s the party was dominated by powerful affiliated unions representing male-dominated heavy industry and manufacturing. The model of the political activist in this party was the male unionized worker; women were defined as wives and mothers, as supporters rather than actors. Their roles were subordinate (Perrigo 1996).

By the 1990s, both changes in the structure of employment and mobilization by party and trade union women led to some reconsideration of the male activist model. Unions began to court women members, and some party modernizers recognized the need to present a less traditional image. A redefinition of equality occurred that enabled women's advocates to make successful gender-based claims. Labour women were therefore able to demand equality both on pragmatic grounds of vote maximization and ideas about justice.

However, difference arguments tended to work against them as class continued to trump gender in hierarchies of diversity.

Liberal Democrat responses to women's claims for equal representation are in some ways the most puzzling. This is a party that historically (as the Liberal Party) favoured the spread of voting rights and embraced rationality. Such beliefs should make the party susceptible to arguments for sex equality. However, there are really two ideologies in the Liberal Democrat Party – classical liberalism and social liberalism. Classical liberalism was dominant for most of the nineteenth century; social liberalism took root after the 1880s. Both strands of liberalism are influential in today's party. Liberals are profound believers in individualism. While classical liberals believe their obligation to individualism is satisfied by the absence of external restraints, social liberals understand that goals of self-realization are thwarted by the inequalities of industrial society, hence intervention in the market may be necessary to adjust outcomes.

In terms of ideas, this division almost exactly mirrors party faultlines over special measures to equalize women's representation, such as quotas. Those who oppose quotas argue that they undermine individualism by demeaning women, denying merit and treating men unfairly. Those who favour quotas believe that change is overdue, that only by intervention in the marketplace of political recruitment will a fair gender balance be achieved. What is odd is that the interventionists, who otherwise dominate the party, appear to lack the power to insist on equality of women's representation. This is in part an organizational artefact whereby constitutional change in the party requires a two-thirds majority vote in party conference – a measure designed to ensure consensus on major changes. Ironically, Liberal Democrat advocates of women's equality have available the ideological resources that come with a belief in egalitarianism. But, perhaps because egalitarianism is so central to their belief system, they also have intrinsic objections to special treatment. In the Liberal Democrat Party, ideas of justice are therefore highly contested, their third party electoral status weakens pragmatic arguments and difference arguments appear only to deepen divisions.

Thus aspects of both ideology and organization are part of the explanations for differences in the way the main British political parties respond to demands for women's political representation. In each party, established sets of ideas are more or less supportive of equality and either favour or oppose intervention. Organizational arrangements reflect divisions that in two of the parties are centred on notions of equality. But claimants for women's equality are latecomers to party politics. Persisting ideological legacies support opposition to their claims and are built into organizations and procedures; they continue to affect attitudes and are capable of impeding women's mobilization.

There are also some constants. Ideology interacts with tradition in all the parties. Success in internal party politics is to a large extent a matter of making alliances among people who can understand and predict each other's behaviour. Gender difference makes two impediments to such alliances. First, women are the unknown 'other'. In Britain, until fairly recently most of the influential classes were educated in single-sex schools and gained public experience in single-sex organizations. Male public leaders had experience of women only in private life. They were unused to women in public life and had no experience or other basis on which to trust them, no habit of making alliances with them. Thus male insiders were particularly inhibited from playing their part in integrating women into politics. However, second, equalization strategies were not viable for the ambitious politician who inevitably feared that women might want special treatment, which might not be good for him.

Political Recruitment

How does party masculinity map onto representation? In most modern democratic systems, political recruitment is the job of political parties. Voters choose among menus of candidates offered by political parties. Social, constitutional, institutional, cultural and political factors constrain those choices in various ways. It is useful to think about obstacles to equal representation in terms of supply and demand. The process of political recruitment is analogous to a market in which the supply consists of those who wish to be representatives, while those who select them determine demand. Demand is affected by the number of available vacancies, perceptions of voter preferences and the attitudes of selectors. Supply is conditioned by the ambitions and motivations of potential candidates and their perceptions of available opportunities. Both are embedded in institutional cultures that produce meanings of political representation and establish the identities and images of appropriate representatives. Resistance is a demand-side constraint, while resources affect both supply and demand. Supply and demand interact in the process of political recruitment. As demand increases, supply expands and vice versa.

It is well established that British voters do not penalize women candidates. The electorate votes for candidates according to party, not sex. In this configuration, the structures that determine candidate selection are crucial. In each party, special rules and procedures determine how candidates are selected. These have been likened to a ladder of recruitment in which different parts of the party exercise vetoes over candidates at each stage of the ascent (Norris and Lovenduski 1995). The precise rules vary in each party. The process begins with eligibility, determined by electoral law, and proceeds through qualification (party membership and experience are normally required) to aspiration, application, nomination, shortlisting and selection stages. In terms of supply, eligible candidates must decide to be party members and then to qualify through a period of activism. They must then apply to be considered as a candidate. Typically, a small committee draws up a shortlist from which members select their candidate. From the point of application, the dynamics of demand predominate.

Political parties differ from each other and vary over time in terms of how the balance of supply and demand factors affect women. Incumbency effects, whereby most MPs expect to keep their seats through several elections, mean that altering the composition of the House of Commons requires continuous effort. British political parties are reluctant to oust incumbents to make space for incomers. The recruitment process is by its very nature a barrier. It is arduous, expensive and frequently disappointing for both women and men. Most applicants fail.

However, there is considerable evidence that aspiring women candidates experience both direct and indirect unfair sex discrimination in all the political parties. Below, I detail the findings of research conducted during 2001 and 2002 on the experiences of women who wished to be candidates and reproduce some of the interviewee responses.[1] The findings illustrate widespread discrimination against women and institutional sexism in the main British political parties.

1 I designed a Fawcett research project that considered the experiences of well-qualified aspirant women candidates who had not been selected for the 2001 general election. In all, 67 women were interviewed for the project, which was conducted with Laura Shepherd Robinson who was then working at Fawcett. Although there was some variation by party, the experience of aspirant women was remarkably similar in all the parties.

This project was designed to enable aspirant women candidates to speak about their selection experiences. Following the 2001 election, Fawcett conducted focus groups with 51 women and telephone interviews with 16 women from the Labour, Conservative, Liberal Democrat and Plaid Cymru parties between July 2001 and February 2002.

Interviewees were well-qualified women candidates who had tried but failed to be selected by a safe or winnable parliamentary constituency for their relevant party for the 2001 election. The first 19 were selected on advice from party activists and further selections were made on a reputational 'snowball' basis. To enable them to speak freely, respondents were seen in party groups and were promised complete confidentiality. The interviews were assessed in the light of the results of the British Representation Study 2001 conducted by Joni Lovenduski and Pippa Norris. See the British Representation Study 2001: <http://www.pippanorris.com>.

The Labour Party

Labour has the most complicated selection procedures. Selection rules are a matter for the party constitution and are intended to be binding on all constituencies. Rules tend to change with each electoral cycle but the basic framework is fairly stable. Nationally, the party maintains a parliamentary panel (list) of approved candidates. Members of this panel are invited to apply for upcoming selections by constituencies which then operate the rest of the procedure. Each constituency consists of various units such as local branches, trade union branches and other affiliated organizations. Each of these units may nominate one candidate to be considered for shortlisting by a general committee.

Prior to the 1999 'Party into Power' organizational reform, women's sections operated at branch level and could make nominations. However, that reform consolidated woman's sections at constituency level, thus reducing the potential for their nominations at branch level because there were fewer women's sections to make nominations.

Selections for the 2001 general election operated as follows. The general committee of the selecting constituency met all nominated candidates and then held a shortlisting meeting. The committee voted on all nominees by single transferable vote. If no sitting MP contested the seat, shortlisting requirements decreed that there should be an equal number of men and women on the shortlist. Shortlisted nominees were then provided with a list of members who were eligible to vote in the final ballot and were entitled to approach those members for support. Voting took place either by postal ballot (applied for in advance) or at a hustings meeting. Often the postal ballot was decisive.

The system of 50/50 men and women on the shortlist of vacant seats replaced the all-women shortlist arrangements of the mid-1990s. It was widely regarded to be a failure. Not only did the 2001 general election return fewer women than in 1997, but also many women thought that the provision was systematically abused. The mechanism was chosen as the least worst option by a Women's Representation Taskforce, which met to make recommendations for selection methods after the 1997 general election. The Taskforce was instructed that all-women shortlists and other quota mechanisms were ruled out for Westminster selections. In practice, the decision may have been worse than nothing, although it did illuminate the continuing resistance to selecting women, and was therefore probably instrumental in the change of policy over quotas after the selection round was completed.

The pitfalls of Labour's 50/50 shortlist policy were all too evident. It became apparent that the device would be used by equality opponents to humiliate and block good women candidates. Labour women were angry and resentful about their selection experiences. They had spent time and money campaigning in seats for which they had been shortlisted. However, at a certain point in the process they came to understand they were not being taken seriously by constituency parties, which had no intention of selecting them. They did not feel that this was because they were not good enough, but because the constituencies had already decided they were going to select a man.

A chap came up and said . . . 'I suppose you are one of the women we have got to look at?'

You find yourself on the short-list but again you are there as a token. You sort of build up this false sense of security.

If you put me on the list that still doesn't do me any good. Why should I be going on the list all the time if I am not going to stand a chance?

One woman also claimed that the 50 per cent requirement was open to abuse due to the fact that the final shortlist had to be gender-balanced. She claimed that in some constituencies, the leading men organized to ensure that the places reserved for women went to those with the fewest local nominations (and therefore the lowest chance of winning) in order to narrow the competition for that seat. Similar allegations were made in the preliminary interviews of party officials and activists that I conducted for the British Representation Study, 2001.

> In some constituencies the women who got the most nominations from branches or unions were not shortlisted because . . . a deal was done to keep the . . . two women with the most nominations off the shortlist. . . . So the only two women that got on the shortlist had one nomination each, so they were never going to beat the men. The men organized to keep the best women off.

Since 1992, the Labour Party has made significant efforts to correct both supply and demand side barriers to the selection of women candidates. However, there is considerable internal division over the policy and many local selectorates resist choosing women candidates. Although the Labour Party has a history of attempting to address discrimination, the perception in many 'individual' cases was that good intentions were not followed through. Discrimination, both overt and covert, reportedly took place throughout the selection process. Moreover, ethnic minority women reported discrimination on grounds of race. Both sexism and racism affected selection processes.

After the 2001 general election, when the numbers of Labour women MPs fell, the government changed the law in order to permit political parties to take special measures, such as creating all-women shortlists to ensure the selection of women candidates. The Labour Party immediately took advantage of the legislation. By March 2004, all-women shortlists had been used in 16 of 26 Labour retirement seats.

However, the policy was contested in parts of the party. In Blaenu Gwent, South Wales, a group of Labour Party constituency officers resigned in protest when it was designated for an all-women shortlist selection. All four of the available Welsh Labour seats selected women. Although Labour was set to lose seats, the early indicators were that their proportion and possibly their numbers of women MPs would rise.

The Conservative Party

Conservative selection operates differently and in some ways resembles recruitment for professional employment. Instead of selection rules, the party issues guidelines to constituencies that include recommended codes of practice to be followed in the selection of candidates. The codes are not always adhered to but it is difficult to complain because they are not binding. The traditional selection process is a series of hurdles that applicants must clear. Hopeful candidates must first apply to be included on an approved list. Their suitability for the list is determined by central office interviews followed by attendance at a weekend selection meeting, where they are judged by experienced party members and officers and MPs. Approved candidates are then notified of upcoming selections by constituency associations.

The final decision is a constituency matter. The CVs of interested candidates are circulated to a constituency candidate selection committee. This committee chooses up to 25 candidates for interview and shortlists between 5 and 7 for interview by the larger Executive Committee of the Constituency Party. Until 2001, the Executive Committee formally met all the candidates on the recommended list then invited them, along with their partners, to a formal interview at which the candidate made a speech and answered questions. The recommended list was then reduced by the Executive Committee to between 2 and 4 people who went forward to a Special General Meeting of members of the association.

Shortlisted candidates made another speech and answered questions at this, often rather large, final selection meeting. Then attending members voted by secret ballot to choose their candidates.

When I observed selection meetings in the Conservative Party during the 1990s I saw that aspirant candidates thought it was very important to present their partners. Unmarried men brought their women partners and referred to them in their speeches. A number of betrothals were announced during the course of a selection process. Constituencies expected to get two people, the candidate and his wife. This expectation offers a means of affirming traditional gender relations. By presenting their women partners, male candidates affirmed their commitment to heterosexual norms and traditional gender relations. When women presented their male spouses, they challenged such traditions.

Much of the traditional selection system is still in place. However, after 2001 there was a debate among some Conservatives who believed the party should be more open to structural change. Party women's advocates mobilized to claim equality of representation. The point has not been won. The problem appears to be one of demand. Since 2001 party leaders have stated that, despite leadership willingness to change, party selectors have continued to be hostile towards women candidates. Despite formal party support for the Sex Discrimination Electoral Candidates Bill in 2001, all-women shortlists have been ruled out. Under the chairmanship of Teresa May, recruitment procedures were scrutinized and overhauled, but stopped short of a real commitment to select women. The party invited equality recruitment expert Jo Sylvester to redesign their recruitment processes to make them more women-friendly. The job description of an MP was formalized in an effort to draw selector attention to the necessary qualifications and to overcome the problem of repeated unthinking selections of favourite sons. In addition, the Conservatives experimented with new selection methods such as the 'open primaries' held at Warrington South and

Reading East in 2004. However, early evidence is that the effects are likely to be limited.

The Conservative women we interviewed were angry about their experiences. They reported many examples of overt discrimination during the 2001 selection round. Selectors failed to observe conventions of equal opportunities, judged women differently from men and were guilty of both sex discrimination and, in some cases, sexual harassment.

> They have no concept of women working. They have no concept of women with children working.

> They always plant this bloody question with a woman to ask it . . . 'What are you going to do about the children?' I thought if this was a job interview I would tell you to mind your own bloody business.

> One chap told me they looked through all these CVs, they had 200 CVs and they didn't interview one woman in the first round . . . he said he turned round to the committee and said 'Don't you think we should have at least a couple of women for a change?' They all looked at him and said it just wasn't an issue for them.

> The male members of the party tend to run a very fine line. Eighty per cent of them don't want you as their MP and 20 per cent of them are actually really nice and really try to help you and a 100 per cent of them want to shag you!

> There is definitely harassment even from people at a very high level. You know, 'Let's go away for the weekend to talk about how I can help you get selected', that kind of thing.

Unlike the Labour Party, Conservatives have a supply problem whereby relatively few women come forward for selection for winnable seats. But the selection experiences of those who do come forward send a message that may well put off potential applicants. To increase its numbers of women MPs, the Conservative Party will need to make changes to its structures and processes. Until recently the Conservatives have not seriously considered how their selection process could be improved to increase the numbers of women selected. Historically, the party defends its selection process (borrowed from British army officer recruitment practices) as 'meritocratic' and has claimed that it 'does not need quotas'.

It is frequently claimed by Conservative Party spokespersons that it is women members who do not want to select women candidates. While there is no reliable systematic evidence that supports this claim, it has been reported so frequently that it has almost become a mantra. In 2001 the Conservatives returned only 14 women MPs, but 92 of their candidates were women. Current party practice is to draw attention to equal opportunity policies and to make provision for equal access to candidate training for women and men. In addition the candidate selection team tries to encourage women to come forward for nomination. In short, the Conservatives continue to rely upon weak policies to support women's selection. Yet such strategies were long ago proved by Labour to be ineffective. At the end of 2003 Fawcett research showed that changes in Conservative candidate selection processes made only a slight difference to women's chances of securing nominations. Of 132 seats by then selected, only 27 were women. Only 2 of 8 retirement seats had by that time selected women. Fawcett predicted that if the Conservatives won 40 new seats in the next general election, only 4 would go to women (Fawcett 2003).

The Liberal Democratic Party

For the 2001 general election, the Liberal Democrats also maintained an approved list from which a local candidate selection committee drew applicants by advertising vacancies. Aspirants applied to the committee. Using agreed selection criteria, up to 10 candidates were invited for interview and at least 3 people were shortlisted. For 2001, shortlists of 3 were required to include at least one man and one woman, and shortlists of 5 had to have at least 2 of each sex. Voting on the final selection took place at a hustings meeting attended by party members.

In contrast to other political parties, overt discrimination was not reported to be a significant problem amongst the Liberal Democrats. This could in part be explained by the their liberal ethos and their formal commitment to tolerance and equality of opportunity. However, covert discrimination did take place and the party is clearly affected by the self-perpetuating male MP model. The shortlist quota was thought to lead to tokenism and both the rural and urban bases of the party were felt to be a disadvantage. Liberal Democrat women reported experiences of unfair discrimination by selectors.

I certainly wouldn't have minded being the 'token woman' *[in a safe Liberal Democrat seat]*. But what I objected to was the three weeks' cost of going down there, moving in and doing all this . . . when they had already decided quite obviously way, way in advance that there was no way a woman was going to do it, that is what I think is wrong.

Unless there is masses and masses of women applicants you do tend to get shortlisted anyway. They always assure you politely that they would have shortlisted you anyway and it is not just because you are the 'token woman' . . . but they had all decided they were going to back *[a now sitting male MP]* . . . what really bugs me is that they didn't bother to tell me . . . I don't think they ought to make use of people like that.

If you go into an industrial area, your members will say to you a woman will never manage in this industrial area . . . and if you go to the rural areas they will say a woman will never do in a rural area, so really we are condemned.

Some Liberal Democrat women thought that the strong preference for 'local' candidates impeded their chances of selection.

> I think my advice for women would be that if you are going to go for a seat, then make sure you were born there, bred there and lived there all your life.

> It's not as easy for women to just up and move everything whereas a lot of men in the party had seen that the selection was going to happen and they moved to the constituency six months before the selection. It's not so easy to do if you're a woman, you're married and you have a family.

> The reason they give you is that they think 'that's the candidate *[the successful candidate]* who the wider electorate, not the party members' ... are going to choose because they're local.

In the 2001 round, Liberal Democrat selectors asked women questions that they did not ask men. One candidate realized she had lost when asked what she would do with her children while campaigning. She replied that, if selected, she would of course have them adopted, an ironic comment that was lost on the selection committee. Our interviews uncovered numerous instances of indirect discrimination, suggesting that, despite efforts to the contrary, equality of opportunity is not consistently operated in the Liberal Democrat selection procedures. Moreover, the shortlisting quota, as in the Labour Party, was not only ineffective but also produced many negative consequences. For Labour and Liberal Democrat women the frequent subversion of the intentions behind quotas on shortlists made a mockery of the efforts made by many qualified women to get selected. As well as dealing with defeat, they had to pay the costs of participation in lengthy procedures even though no one had any intention of selecting them.

Measures to increase the selection of women candidates are a continuing issue for the Liberal Democrats. The 2001 party conference rejected a motion to use all-women shortlists in party seats and in target seats. Instead they opted for weaker measures such as the provision of training and support for women candidates. A Gender Balance Task Force was established to direct their efforts. By the end of 2003, 40 of the 110 Liberal Democratic candidates already selected were women. Because the Liberal Democrats select their best seats early, this number may portend an improvement, as it is a significant increase on the 22 per cent selected for 2001. Candidate selection is ongoing and it may be that these improvements do not hold up. Moreover, by the end of 2003 only one woman had been selected to fight a party retirement seat but one woman MP announced that she would retire. Even if the early pattern of selecting more women continues, the electoral fortunes of the Liberal Democrats do not promise a massive contribution to an increase in the overall numbers of women MPs (Fawcett 2004).

However, by stepping back from quotas, Liberal Democrats are attempting to demonstrate that in their equality-minded party, such measures are unnecessary to progress towards balanced representation of women and men. It may be that the combination of political will and egalitarian ethos will ensure continued progress to sex equality. However, this will mean an enormous change in the party's selection habits. A struggle is taking place in this party that merits the attention of equality advocates and experts. Many party women are unconvinced by soft measures, hence demands for quotas continue to be raised.

Common Obstacles

In all three parties the barriers to women's selection could be explained by institutional sexism. In addition, becoming a candidate is an expensive process. Women not only have fewer resources with which to cover these costs; they also include additional costs, with fewer sources of support.

> I do have to pay the bills and so certainly I think in seats where, for example, men have been supported by their unions and given time off to go and do that, that is very important.

> The other thing that has to change quite radically is the amount of money that can be spent on campaigning ... some people will be spending £800 on a glossy leaflet whereas I would be spending £11 printing it myself ... you automatically preclude those mothers who are at home who just don't have the money to pay the child care, the petrol, the stationery, the £500 stamps that you have to do to leaflet.

> Men are still paid better then women and a lot of these male candidates were from London ... so they were even more well paid than the average woman. It is a very, very expensive process. Even doing it as cheaply as you possibly can, you are talking thousands of pounds to run a campaign knowing that as a woman you are not going to get there.

> It must be probably one of the few elections in this country where you can actually spend precisely what you want on this. I think that is something that does need looking at.

In all three parties women reported that they were judged on a different basis from men. They reported numerous examples of overt discrimination, ranging from traditional assumptions about their roles to outright and explicit discrimination including sexual harassment. In each party the procedures offer numerous opportunities for the overt expression of selector preferences for white male candidates even where rules explicitly prohibit unfair discrimination. Our interviews uncovered examples of sexual harassment in both the Labour and the Conservative parties. For example, in the Conservative Party:

[A Conservative woman going for selection in a safe seat] was asked . . . 'if she got *[the seat]* and was in Westminster during the week, what would her husband do for sex?'

I was talking to a group of people *[involved in the selection in which I was unsuccessful]* and I was telling a story . . . of how I unusually had spent the whole night awake thinking about it . . . this chap said to me, he was in his sixties, he looked as though he had parked his Range Rover outside and his wellies were still in the boot, and he said to me 'yes, I lay awake all night thinking about you too' . . . I knew in any other environment I would have said 'how dare he speak to me like that'.

I am not a very PC sort of person but I really do believe that women should not be subjected to that *[sexual harassment]*, they wouldn't get away with it in the workplace nowadays.

The main thing I would do differently next time is to learn how to say 'no' *[to offers of sex]* without making enemies.

Labour appears not to have been much better:

They are absolutely adamant they will not consider a woman . . . it was said to me . . . 'we do enjoy watching you speak, we always imagine what your knickers are like'. It is that basic. 'We picture you in your underwear when you are speaking.' That is what you are dealing with.

There are small groups within the party who come out with the most outrageous comments. But the very fact that these comment are made and with any regularity . . . that they go unchallenged is quite staggering in this day and age.

Sexism and Racism

Institutional sexism was compounded by racism. Minority ethnic women experienced additional problems in both the Labour and Conservative parties. Labour women reported experience of overt racism:

> There are people in the local parties and at constituency level who will say they won't have a woman or a black person.

> Ordinary party members still have this stereotype that what makes an MP is a white male.

> When it comes to selection you have got 51–80-year olds. How can you change the mind of that man? They are probably not dealing with black people a lot. They don't deal with women a lot. They have a perception from 50 years ago that a man is the guy to do the job.

> There is a group of people in the party . . . who will not want a woman; will not want a black woman.

They also reported problems they attributed to ill-formed policies to contest racism in the party. The ethnic minority women interviewed said that in the same way that women in general were always on shortlists but very rarely got selected for winnable seats, they found it incredibly easy to get on shortlists but they felt they were there merely as 'tokens' without any real chance of getting selected.

> They make certain there is a black minority ethnic person on the final shortlist. That has actually worked against us. All the time you find yourself on the shortlist but you are there as a token.

> They called all the people who had gone for that seat of ethnic origin and they called us all into this fabulous

room in Millbank. They had the press and all these
eminent MPs . . . and it was all a farce. It was all for one
[male] individual . . . I felt I was totally violated, used,
abused, I was so upset afterwards.

It is all lip service. It is saying we want more black and
Asian people in. You can't get them in if it is only lip
service. You need a mechanism to make it happen.

We are there to make the list look good as black women.

Most of the ethnic minority Conservative women interviewed said they had been extremely reluctant to acknowledge that racism was a factor in their failure to get selected.
However, after having been through the selection process
many times, this was precisely the conclusion they were
coming to.

What they want is a nice, young white boy who they
can see marrying their granddaughter.

If they can't see you in their social environment, they
don't want to select you.

I've looked at everything else and there isn't another
reason. It could be they just don't like me, but then how
do you differentiate between they don't like me, and
they don't like me because I'm brown?

In both the Labour and Conservative parties, ethnic minority women face additional discrimination. Sex and race
discrimination interact in candidate selection processes so that
well-qualified women repeatedly fail to be selected. Moreover, a compounded tokenism may ensure that minority
ethnic women are shortlisted only to be rejected by selection
committees.

Especially in the Labour Party, but also in the Conservative and Liberal Democrat parties there were frequent

accusations that procedures were not followed, that advant-ages were given to some candidates. For Labour and Liberal Democrat women the repeated subversion of the intentions behind quotas on shortlists made a mockery of the efforts made by many qualified women to get selected.

Summary of Obstacles

In all three parties women's selection was found to be impeded by institutional sexism, which in the Labour and Conservative parties was frequently compounded by racism.[2] Barriers to the feminization of politics are institutionalized into the political organizations in which representation takes place. These barriers can be summarized as amounting to institutional sexism and racism which support particular kinds of white masculinity in political organizations, manifested in its personnel, procedures and policies. In the British case, sexism seems especially well insulated and can be seen to operate in both Parliament and the political parties. It is worth noting that the Victorian ideals of heterosexual masculinity, so prevalent in UK political imagery, is specific to the polit-ical culture (though there is evidence that it was exported to the empire.) Such traditional attitudes to women's roles take a number of forms and are frequently an impediment to women's representation (Norris 2004). They are most visible on the demand side of political recruitment but may also, as in the case of the Conservative Party, affect supply.

Many of the barriers and obstacles to women were com-mon in all the main parties. Labour, the Liberal Democrats and the Conservatives all reported overt discrimination, the lack of a genuine culture of equal opportunities, greater financial constraints for women than for men, tokenism,

2 We were unable to interview ethnic minority women from the Liberal Democratic Party. The Liberal Democratic women we interviewed did not mention race discrimination.

'favourite sons' and the syndrome of the self-perpetuating male stereotype whereby safe constituencies tend to try to reproduce the MP they have always had who may have been selected 30 years previously.

To some extent, barriers are a manifestation within the parties of the disadvantages experienced by women in society at large. Change may follow the entry of new generations of party members. Party members vary by age in their willingness to nominate women candidates. Older party members of both sexes in all parties are reported to hold traditional views of women's roles; hence, they prefer their MP to be a man. But such reactions are compounded by the party cultures that have institutionalized codes of behaviour that make discrimination against women both possible and acceptable.

In addition, the Conservative Party has both supply and demand problems (few of those few women who do come forward are nominated for winnable seats) especially in target seats or seats where a Conservative MP retires. Labour and the Liberal Democrats have demand problems. In all the parties supply and demand interact. Labour's experience shows that as demand increases, women are more likely to come forward.

Under pressure from feminist advocates, all three parties have at various times acknowledged the problem of women's underrepresentation. All three have made attempts to increase the presence of women in Parliament. Their efforts have had varying success. Neither Conservative nor Liberal Democrat women have made much progress at national level. In the Conservative Party especially, efforts by leaders to expand women's representation have met with selector resistance. Leaders continue to be reluctant to impose the kinds of measure that will bring change, claiming that party members would not comply. Liberal Democrats support equality of representation in formal terms but are divided over the means. Advocates of change have been unable to secure support for effective special measures. Labour has had more success but has also been more determined. In 2001 Labour introduced compulsory special measures at the actual point of selection, thus mandating the selection of minimum numbers of women. However, Labour incumbents are protected by their selection policies, which reduces the number of vacancies available to women.

Nevertheless, however tentatively, all three parties have embarked on a long-term change that has the potential to transform their cultures, images and possibly their fortunes. The variations between the parties are large. Whilst the Labour Party has apparently been able to step over its institutional sexism and take the risks of selecting more women by compulsory measures, the other parties are more hesitant. The Liberal Democrats still seem to be ambivalent, while the Conservatives, if they do favour equality, are cautious almost to the point of paralysis. These differences reflect varying obstacles to equality of women's political representation that are explained by party ideology, organization and leadership. They are also affected by variations in the mobilization of party women for change, a process discussed in more detail in chapter 5.

4

Equality Strategies and the Quota Movement

What strategies are available to feminists seeking political equality? Some years ago, Vicky Randall (1982) suggested that the safest option would be to move to Sweden. Although she was joking, she had a point. In terms of political representation, Sweden has come closer to a feminist politics than any other country. Although Swedish women are quick to point out that there are numerous remaining gender inequalities in their system, they seem from the vantage point of rather backward England to have the problems of the privileged. Another possibility would have been to design the political system and its institutions properly in the first place. Feminist research offers some indications of how this could now be done. The creation of gender-balanced institutions elected on the basis of party list proportional representation systems of election, combined with arrangements that public-appointed offices are filled according to non-sexist criteria of qualifications, would be central to such systems. Candidate lists would not be allowable unless they contained an equal number of women and men, ordered in such a way that they had equal chances of election. Principles of rotation would be guaranteed. Government positions, including those of president and prime minister, would alternate between women and men.

Where monarchs were heads of state, women would have equal rights of succession to men and genetic engineering would be used to ensure that succession alternated between the sexes.

Feminists have not, to my knowledge, designed such utopian systems. Most equality advocates try to reform their political systems rather than to create completely new states. But the feminization of established political procedures and institutions has proved to be a long and frustrating process. In practice, equality advocates in established democracies normally confront political institutions that have been around for some time. There are exceptions to this, of course. New institutions are sometimes designed following constitutional change or political transition. Such initiatives offer opportunities to build in requirements for women's presence. I return to this point below.

Although the obstacles to equality of representation for women in established political institutions are formidable, they have been overcome in many states and are being effectively challenged in others. Equality advocates in democratic systems have available a considerable strategic repertoire. Women claiming equality have both generated and engaged in debates about political representation and constitutional change and other debates about institutional design. They have mobilized in local, national and international social movements, and within established political organizations such as parties, trade unions and professional organizations. This was a long process of political learning that established strategic resources for advocates who frequently borrowed tactics from sister organizations. In this process, treaties, constitutions, procedures, formal and informal rules and daily practices have been affected.

The best opportunities to affect decisions come at the point of the establishment of political institutions; a point well recognized in Scotland, where feminists were determined to be involved at every stage of the constitution-making process. Constitution-making was a protracted operation in which participation was motivated by an act of faith, by a belief that devolution would happen and that equality advocates would be able to influence the shape of the settlement. After the Scotland Bill failed in the 1970s, because the enabling referendum did not win the required number of votes, a campaign for a Scottish Assembly was established to keep the issue on the political agenda. For the next 25 years campaigns and organizations to establish an assembly continued. Aiming to gain wide popular agreement for constitutional change, campaigners used a variety of tactics. Central to their approach was working with advocates in many of the political parties and making alliances with the social partners and civic and voluntary associations.

Feminists, many of them political party members, intervened in this process to become part of the movement for change. They sought a Scottish legislature in which women held 50 per cent of the places and were well represented in its cabinet and executive. Under the umbrella of the Scottish Women's Co-ordination Group, they lobbied the Constitutional Convention and the political parties to gender the debate. They drew attention to the kind of electoral system that would most benefit women and secured agreement from Labour and Liberal Democrat Party leaders to elect women candidates. As the prospects for devolution became more promising, equality advocates became involved in discussions about institutional design. They argued that it would be necessary in order to avoid the adversarial culture of Westminster and to establish a Parliament that would facilitate consensual ways of making policy. Criticism of the nature of English government went down well in Scotland.

The achievement of feminist advocates in Scotland was considerable. The Labour Party agreed to a quota system (twinning: see chapter 5) which, in the first elections, returned 28 women and 28 men to the new Parliament. The Scottish National Party did almost as well, electing 15 women and 20 men. When the first Scottish Parliament opened for business, 37 per cent of its members were women. In its first executive, women were 30 per cent of ministers and took 41 per cent of the committee places, including 6 out of 17 convenorships (Brown et al. 2002). Its blueprint included arrangements for inclusive consensual and cooperative ways of doing business. This was a process that involved classic political strategies. Engagement in debate, an understanding of the rules of the game, the mobilization of support, the formation of alliances, the remaking of political discourse and the accumulation and dissemination of expertise all operated to affect the rules of the game. The women's 'Claim of Right' was successful because there was a widespread and well-established movement that was integrated into political organizations and institutions able not only to insert feminist claims into the growing momentum for change but also to make those claims seem crucial to success. Their demands were strengthened by feminist mobilization in the Labour Party and by the need to make a successful coalition for devolution in Wales, where the policy had attracted less enthusiasm and women's equality advocates were welcome supporters.

In both countries, the absence of incumbents was an important opportunity for feminists. Once an institution is established and incumbents are installed, the stakes are raised. In both Scotland and Wales the number of women representatives increased in the second round of elections. The increases occurred partly because incumbency status gave women a strong starting point and partly because quotas were used by some political parties in the second rounds. In 2003 women made up 40 per cent of members of the Scottish Parliament and 50 per cent of members of the Welsh National Assembly.

This example illustrates well the strategies available to women claiming equality of political representation, albeit in a situation of unusually good opportunity. Scottish women did not become political men to make their claims. What they did was disrupt old alliances, challenge prevailing discourses and offer practical feminized solutions to real obstacles in the way of devolution. They became part of a political process as a way of transforming it.

Scotland was an unusual opportunity, as devolution took place in a small, highly politicized country in which feminists were well mobilized and networked. Transition periods create opportunities in which women's claims for equality may potentially be integrated into reformed or new political systems. There are no guarantees that feminization will result, however. Women fared less well in the transitions in Eastern Europe where there was little feminist mobilization at the time of institutional change. Numbers of women went down dramatically in foundational elections (Matland and Montgomery 2003). Nor do all constitution-making processes create opportunities for women. The mobilization to include gender equality in the concerns of the European Constitution proved difficult.

Opportunities to make claims for equality of representation are especially evident in times of constitutional change, but routine politics may also be susceptible to intervention. Advocates can generate debate by drawing attention to shortfalls in a system's representation of women. They can mobilize feelings of national pride by drawing attention to comparisons with other countries. They can campaign for governments to sign up to and then implement international agreements on women's representation. They can draw on national discourses of freedom and equality to advance feminist claims and draw on discourses of difference to claim special treatment of various kinds. This raises the question of how much representation feminists should claim. One possibility is to claim all available representation until women have achieved half of all positions. This goal is predicated not only on a simple notion of descriptive representation, but also on perceptions about how many women it will take to transform the culture of an institution, an issue discussed in chapter 6.

How Should the Claims be Made?

Feminists are frequently divided over the question of whether to work within or outside an existing political system. Such divisions are part of the politics of achieving equality of women's representation. They often find expression in sustained debates among feminists and between feminists and others about the meaning of political representation and the appropriateness of the use of insider and outsider strategies for excluded or marginal groups. It is difficult to assess these debates because it is difficult to establish agreement about what constitutes a good outcome. If we assume that sustained and substantial increases in the numbers of women representatives are necessary to the feminization of politics, then insider strategies are essential. However, insider strategies work better when an autonomous women's movement is present in the system and active on the issue (Lovenduski et al. 2005).

Effective organization is necessary but not sufficient. Historically feminists adopted institutional strategies, working within parties and accepting existing rules of the game. The example of Scotland shows how important it is for feminists to be mobilized ahead of decisions about change. Moreover, change may be very slow. In the contrasting example of the United States, after many years of campaigns for equal representation, women's presence was comparatively low at 14 per cent of the Senate and 14 per cent of the House of Representatives in 2003. Yet by the beginning of the twentieth century, women's advocates had been active in the main American political parties. Jo Freeman (2000) describes a pattern of long periods of slow increase in the numbers and status of party women, followed by a brief but sharp rise, then a brief decline and a resumption of the long slow increase. Two main strategies were pursued: getting women onto party committees and creating special political clubs for women. The history is marked by generational shifts, major disputes and significant achievement.

Equality Strategies and the Quota Movement

The USA example offers an illustration of how the feminization of politics depends on the nature of the parties, the opportunity structure of the times and the surrounding women's movement. For a few years after American women won the suffrage in each state, efforts were made to seek out women to run for office, but such efforts were always short-lived. In the USA the lack of party competition in most places during and after the campaign for women's suffrage may have meant that parties had no incentive to alter their patterns of candidate selection. Freeman argues that women's claims for equality of representation were undermined by the fact that by the time women's suffrage was won, extensive areas of one party dominance made it unnecessary for parties to court women's votes.

The otherwise contrasting examples of Scotland and the USA both suggest that increases in women's representation require feminist advocacy and the support of political parties. In most democratic systems, political parties monopolize political representation and take the important decisions about who the representatives will be. Successful advocacy requires a moment when parties are seeking new constituencies, although, as the example of the British Conservative Party after 1997 suggests, this is not a sufficient condition. The nature of the political system inevitably affects how claims for representation are made. Here again, distinctions between justice, pragmatic and difference arguments may illuminate appropriate strategies. Once the justice argument is made and has gained some acceptance, it is easier to consider ways of correcting imbalances in representation and then generate debate about how best to do this.

The adoption of strategies to increase women's political representation in modern democracies is a process in which ideas about justice are invoked as the basis for political equality. The process is not necessarily linear in the short term, but over time it is possible to observe some progression. How does the process work? The key actors are advocacy organizations, political parties and social movements, which interact and may overlap, as the claims of advocates in all three become more insistent. The actors, as organizations of groups and individuals, are diverse. The organizations are themselves arenas of change. They contain opponents and supporters both of equality of women's representation and of different means to achieve it. To illuminate the process, it is useful to explicate the available strategies, the debates that surround them and to discuss the way they play out in various contexts.

Broadly, there are three available strategies: equality rhetoric, equality promotion or positive action and equality guarantees or positive discrimination. Equality rhetoric is the public acceptance of women's claims. It is found in party campaign platforms and party political discourse and the speeches and writing of political leaders. Equality rhetoric means words and arguments are spoken and written that may well impact on attitudes and beliefs. In some cases the rhetoric incorporates feminist discourse and through subtle but significant shifts in language makes other strategies seem possible. For example, governments have agreed to international treaties and protocols calling for equality of women's and men's representation. Initiated by feminists working in the international movements, documents such as the United Nations Platform for Action express equality claims in feminist terms. Such documents have subsequently been used as a basis for domestic mobilization in support of sex equality. The language in which they are framed gains legitimacy partly as a result of its treaty or protocol status and begins to be used in public debate, to be reported in the mass media and to frame political thinking and argument. Through such processes an equality discourse emerges that may increase the common ground for action.

However, rhetorical strategies stop short of policies for change. Equality promotion attempts to bring women into political competition by offering special training and financial assistance, and setting targets for women's presence and other measures to enable women to come forward. In European party democracies the arguments must first be won in political parties, which then take the ideas into government. Governments have funded awareness campaigns, made financial assistance available for positive action programmes, funded women's advocacy organizations, funded research on women's representation, included women's advocacy organizations in consultations at all levels, signed international treaties and protocols calling for equality of women's and men's representation, made provision to ensure that women were appointed to public office, removed legal obstacles to women's representation, removed legal obstacles to special measures to promote women's equality and reserved seats for women in legislatures. However, not all governments are in a position to deliver equality. In European party democracies it is essential to work through political parties. Parties in such systems necessarily have some autonomy; hence, government action is often permissive rather than decisive. Equality promotion aims to bring more women into politics through encouragement and by facilitating their ability to compete in various ways. It is directed mainly at the supply of potential representatives.

Equality guarantees or positive discrimination treats the *demand* for women representatives. In such strategies places are reserved for women on electoral slates and in representative bodies. Quotas, discussed below at length, are examples of equality guarantees. Using quotas, parties and governments secure places for women representatives by making their sex a necessary qualification for office. Such policies are controversial; however, they are increasingly used. Policies to increase women's presence may be permissive, voluntary or compulsory and they may offer opportunities or guarantees. Permissive policies remove formal obstacles to women's representation such as legal exclusions. They may also remove prohibitions on the use of voluntary or compulsory policies. An example is the UK's Sex Discrimination (Electoral Candidates) Act of 2002, which permits parties to use positive discrimination in the selection of their electoral candidates.

Since the 1960s political parties, under pressure from their women members, have made regular pronouncements about the need to have more women leaders and have adopted awareness-raising campaigns to highlight women's under-representation. Such rhetorical strategies assume or pretend that the omission of women is an unintended or undesired consequence of the current political arrangements that will be corrected as soon as the error is pointed out. They are often unsuccessful until measures are taken to bring women into the candidate selection process at all levels of the political system. When successful, equality rhetoric draws attention to women's underrepresentation, which creates continuing opportunities for women's advocates to mobilize around women's representation demands. Such mobilization occurs both inside and outside political parties. For example, feminists within parties draw attention to demands for inclusion by autonomous women's movements. In response to such demands, parties have developed measures to enlarge the pool of eligible women through training and education programmes to ensure that sufficient numbers of eligible women are available. In general, increasing the supply of women has resulted in only small gains in representation. However, the presence of a more than adequate supply of women has highlighted the resistance to women candidates and brought into sharp relief the need for policies to increase demand. On such a reading, the adoption of equality rhetoric by a political party or government may portend a sequence of events whereby, once spoken, the promise of sex equality sets off a process that continues until equal representation is delivered.

Quotas

Scrutiny of modern European democracies bears out my account of the processes of mobilizing for equality of women's political representation. Sex equality advocates mobilized for and won equality guarantees from political parties and more recently from legislatures. Beyond those largely similar systems, a worldwide explosion in the use of candidate quotas has occurred. Women candidate quotas are now a global phenomenon. More than 100 countries have experienced debates on the issue; more than 80 of them have adopted quotas of women candidates. These developments have been accompanied by an explosion of research into the politics of such quotas that suggests considerable diversity in terms of both the form they take and their effectiveness (Baldez 2004; Dahlerup 2002; Htun and Jones 2002; IDEA 2002; IDEA 2003; Krook 2003; Matland and Studlar 1996; Norris 2004).

There is not space here for a full discussion of the patterns and uses of quotas. Instead, in the remainder of this chapter I will first introduce briefly the politics of quotas to make general points about their increasing use as a mechanism to engineer equality of women's political representation. I will then argue that quota debates are significantly affected by the institutional and political context in which they occur. By this I mean that the same mechanism may work quite differently in one system from how it does in another.

Any discussion of quotas first requires that we address at least seven related questions.

1 What are candidate quotas?
2 What forms do they take?
3 When and where are quotas adopted?
4 Who supports quotas and why?
5 Who opposes quotas and why?
6 How effective are quotas at increasing women's political representation?
7 What explains differences in their effectiveness?

What are Quotas?

Political quotas are regulations that a certain number or proportion of women (in this case) must be present in a representative forum or institution. They may operate at different stages of the selection process, with political parties, at the nomination stage, or as a requirement for the composition of a legislature, assembly, council or government.

The main types of quota are reserved seats, legal quotas and quotas stipulated in party rules. Some countries formally reserve a share of seats for women in their legislatures. Examples are Bangladesh, Botswana, Pakistan, Taiwan and Tanzania. Legal quotas specify that all political parties must nominate a certain minimum number of women candidates. Examples include France, Argentina and Costa Rica. Party quotas are the most common (Norris 2004: ch. 8). They take the form of internal party requirements to nominate at least a minimum number of women for elected office. Party quotas are sometimes described in gender-neutral terms; hence, they may prescribe a minimum of candidates of both sexes. (see <www.idea.int/quota>). They operate on the supply side of political representation by inviting potential candidates into the process of selection. However, their most significant effect is on the demand side, because they stipulate that there should be a certain presence of women among candidates and/or in office.

Each type of quota is supported by implementation requirements that may be more or less effective. Although the point of all three types is to increase the presence of women, the question of whether they offer rhetoric, promotion or guarantees of equality depends upon the details of their requirements and particularly upon the sanctions that are used in the event of non-compliance (Dahlerup and Freidenvall 2003).

When and Where are Quotas Used?

Quotas have been used to place women in political office for some time. Pakistan first implemented reserved seats for women in 1956 and Bangladesh did so in the 1970s (IDEA 2003). By the end of 2003, examples of quotas of women candidates were to be found in all major world regions and in all governmental and party system types. They occurred under various dominant religions and in countries at differing levels of human development. In 2003, 14 countries used or had used constitutional quotas of women for national parliaments and 31 used or had used electoral quotas at national level. A further 17 countries had quotas of some kind at sub-national level (Krook 2003; see also <www.idea.int/quota>).

Who Supports Quotas and Why?

In some cases compulsory quotas were introduced because other strategies had failed and support for more stringent requirements grew as it became evident that voluntary measures were not working. Many advocates of compulsory quotas once believed they were unjustified and came only reluctantly to the conclusion that there was no alternative if women were to win politically meaningful representation. But there may be other reasons for the adoption of quotas. Guarantees of reserved places for women may be a way of appeasing but at the same time sidelining women's advocates, or demonstrating a commitment to women's rights that is not actually present. Where the reserved places are filled by appointment, the women may lack the popular base that would give them any real say in decision-making (Norris 2004: ch. 8).

According to Krook (2003: 21–2), quota advocates include some women's movement organizations, women's sections inside political parties, women leaders, some national leaders, transnational equality networks and international and cross-national networks of women's movements, parts of the judiciary and/or women leaders. In Western Europe the typical alliance of quota advocates is between women's sections in political parties, women's movements and women in party elites and in government (Caul 1999; Krook 2003). This is the alliance that featured in British quota politics.

The most widely used argument for quotas is that they are effective. They make political institutions responsible for ensuring the representation of women and, used over a period of time, normalize women's presence. They reduce the pressure on incoming women who benefit from being part of a larger group. Many of their supporters argue that quotas are a necessary compensation for systems that have deprived women of a presence in politics. This argument draws on the theoretical cases (justice and difference) for women's representation and justifies quotas as the only means to ensure it. Institutionalists argue that quotas are part of a process that brings women into all parts of the political system and sets in train further processes that will ensure that their presence continues. There are many motivations that affect supporters of quotas. Some advocates are motivated by their beliefs that gender balance in decision-making is justified at any price. Electoral considerations are also a strong motivator. International pressures may require elites to speed up their processes of integrating women. For example, prospective entrants to the European Union may wish to increase women's representation in an effort to display their democratic credentials. Finally, quotas have sometimes been introduced by representatives of international institutions in post-conflict societies such as Afghanistan, Iraq and Kosovo. Such decisions result both from domestic pressures by women in participating countries and internal pressures from women in the countries in which they are installed. They are a reflection of changing norms across societies according to which gender balance in decision-making is ever more regarded as an important component of regime legitimacy (Htun and Jones 2002; Krook 2003).

Who Opposes Quotas and Why?

In Western Europe the main opponents of quotas have been the courts, some politicians (of both sexes) and some political parties. Male incumbents may have a strong interest in resisting quotas and an ability to act against them, which is why arrangements frequently protect incumbents, thus delaying implementation. Male politicians have used the courts to overturn quota decisions. On occasion, international organizations have refused to institute quotas. An example is East Timor, where calls by UNIFEM (UN Development Fund for Women) and local activists to institute a quota of women were rejected by the UN Electoral Assistance Division in New York. According to Krook (2003) the UN Division did not want to set a precedent for UN supervised elections.

Probably the most powerful argument against quotas is that they risk essentialism. Critics claim quotas invoke the essential category of women and marginalize other differences. The election of 37 per cent women to the Scottish Parliament and 40 per cent women to the Welsh Assembly in 1999, but no members from ethnic minorities, may be evidence of such an effect. Liberal theories of representation support arguments that quotas are unfair to men, who should not be excluded on grounds of sex. Another argument that has resonance with feminists is that concentration on quotas may obscure larger questions of political transformation. This argument suggests that quotas are a way of working within the existing system of political institutions that fails to challenge the effects of institutions on gender identity.

The example of Uganda illustrates the problem. Ugandan women have guaranteed representation in their legislature. However, gendered regulations and customs governing public behaviour mean they are not able to go to restaurants with men. Yet male politicians retire from the assembly to restaurants to do the bargaining that is part of legislative politics (Dahlerup and Squires 2002; Krook 2003). This is not an isolated example. Despite high levels of representation of women in politics, the Nordic countries feature the most segregated labour markets in Europe. Nor are such problems new. In the nineteenth and twentieth centuries European feminist campaigners for women's representation struggled to move political meetings and ballots from bars, pubs and other men-only spaces.

Other anti-quota arguments are that they risk backlash by otherwise supportive male incumbents and hopefuls; they risk recruiting unqualified women just because they are women, which will deprive electors of adequate representation; women thus selected may be stigmatized and therefore less powerful and effective in the legislature; the men responsible for political recruitment will nominate women who are more compliant. Finally, politics may become polarized on gender lines. These are reasonable arguments, but, with the exception of the last one, are no more than possible temporary effects that will disappear as women's political presence is normalized and the process of representation continues. Moreover, the argument that guarantees of women's presence polarizes politics on gender lines may actually be a case for quotas, as it suggests that there are gendered interests to be represented.

How Effective are Quotas?

The short answer to this question is that much depends on the mechanism that is employed, the mobilization of party women and the determination of political leaders. The choice of mechanism is related to the electoral system. The arguments about the impact of electoral systems on women's political representation have been usefully summarized by Pippa Norris. In her account, the effects are fairly clear. Worldwide, more women get elected under party list proportional representation systems than under majoritarian systems. In 2003, women made up 8.5 per cent of MPs in majoritarian systems and 15.4 per cent under proportional systems. However, there was a significant variation within each group. The variations could be explained by institutional and social factors. The most important institutional variations were differences in district magnitude and proportionality, type of party system, party ideology and the use of quotas of women (Norris 2004).

Equality Strategies and the Quota Movement

Women benefit from proportional representation party list systems because, first, parties presenting lists have an incentive to present socially balanced slates of candidates to the electorate; it makes them 'look' more representative. Second, incumbency effects are slightly weaker, therefore a few more vacancies are generated. Third, party lists facilitate quotas because they offer more opportunities to include women without excluding men, while in single member constituencies where parties may nominate only one candidate parties must choose between women and men.

Norris's analysis demonstrates that the presence of a favourable electoral system is neither a necessary nor a sufficient condition for achieving high levels of women's representation. Social factors, which she summarizes in terms of levels of economic development, play a considerable part. It appears that electoral system effects are strongest in post-industrial societies and weakest in developing countries (Norris 2004).

The form that quotas take depends on the institutional and cultural context that in turn determines the available sanctions. Comparative research suggests that the type of electoral and party system affects not only the kind of quotas that are adopted, but also their likelihood of being implemented. Closed lists and high district magnitude favour effective (in the sense of delivering more women representatives) implementation (Htun and Jones 2002). Implementation depends upon party compliance, which in turn depends on normative attitudes and the calculations that leaders make about the benefits of compliance in relation to the costs of non-compliance. Where not implemented, quotas may simply be another kind of equality rhetoric, part of the process but not yet a solution.

Examples of the use of quotas show how institutionally constrained or path-dependent is the form that they take. In Western Europe, quotas are part of a repertoire of measures designed to enhance women's political representation. The Scandinavian countries are a case in point, and it is there that women have achieved the highest levels of political

99

representation in modern democracies. Political parties in Denmark, Norway and Sweden used quota provisions in the 1980s to increase women's political representation. By that time, women already constituted between 20 and 30 per cent of legislators. Although the introduction of quotas led to further increases, a significant breakthrough had already taken place (Dahlerup and Friedenvall 2003). In these countries equality promotion led to the building of political capacity so that women, once elected, were able to operate effectively, not least to promote further increases in the political representation of women. Dahlerup and Friedenvall (2003) refer to this model as the 'incremental track' and note that its implementation meets strong male resistance.

These authors have recently argued that the gradual improvement in women's political representation of the equality-minded Nordic states is no longer an option. Women are claiming political representation and demanding quotas to secure it without waiting for secularization to take place or welfare states to develop or democratic stability to make gradual increases in presence possible. Hence a fast-track model has emerged globally. Advocates of fast-track quotas refuse gradual improvement. Their rationale is that exclusion itself is the problem, so that inclusion is the obvious solution. The strategy concentrates on simply defined outcomes (more women representatives) and does not guarantee that capacity-building will accompany the increased presence of women (Dahlerup and Friedenvall 2003). Norris's account, described above, fits well with Dahlerup's and Freidenvall's arguments about incremental and fast-track arrangements for women's political representation. The incidence of fast-track quotas is now widespread. Frequently, such measures are adopted in democratizing systems. The examples of South Africa, where ANC women demanded and obtained quotas so that over 30 per cent of the founding legislature were women, and of Latin America, where democratizing parties have established quotas of women, are cases in point. However, the democratizing systems of Eastern and Central Europe offer a counter-example. There, the routine inclusion of substantial percentages of women in powerless legislatures by discredited regimes left campaigners for women's presence in politics without an acceptable strategy for implementing their claims during crucial post-transition elections. Later, quotas were adopted in Bosnia and Herzegovina, Croatia, Hungary, Poland, Romania, Slovakia and Slovenia (<www.idea.int/quota>). The East European example shows that quotas not only have opponents but they also have disadvantages (Matland and Montgomery 2003).

Quota Strategies Assessed

Quota debates are practical matters that invite pragmatic arguments. At one time associated with the left, there are now many examples of centre and right-wing parties adopting quotas of women candidates (Guadagnini 2005; Norris 2004). Quotas are about power, not coherence. They are also context-specific, affected by the discourses and cultures of the systems in which arguments must be made. Hence, arguments for and against quotas do not operate on the same intellectual/theoretical terrain as arguments about democratic representation. Arguments about the former tend to be long term and universal, whilst strategic arguments about quotas are shorter term and particular. They are frequently pragmatic and their appearance is associated with electoral cycles, party fortunes and constitutional change.

In general, quotas for women are intended to give women more power. However, to introduce quotas against severe resistance 'requires that women have already gained some power' (Dahlerup 1998). A number of issues are raised by the politics of quotas. Many of these parallel or derive from debates about women's presence. First is the question of why male-dominated institutions and parties should implement quotas. Second is the issue of 'quota women'. Who are they, are they distinguishable from other elected women, are they subject to some stigmatization and what parts of their experiences are temporary and transitional, what parts are more lasting? Third is the relationship of quotas to the social structure. Feminist advocates have expected that increased representation of women would somehow lead to increased representation by other groups. This is an important and controversial claim that needs to be considered carefully and, where quotas are in place, tested empirically. Fourth, institutional design is significant. To be effective, a quota must be suited to the system in which it is installed, as the UK and French examples vividly demonstrate.

In many countries quotas are adopted as symbols of democratic representation in what are otherwise less than democratic states. CEDAW (Convention on the Elimination of Discrimination Against Women) has been important to such decisions; hence quotas have been implemented in systems in which women do not have equal social rights. In 2001 Pakistan introduced 33 per cent quotas for women at municipal level. In some Arab countries the quota system is used to get token and controllable women on board, while claiming that they promote women's representation. In Uganda a parliamentary seat from each of 39 districts is reserved for women. In Argentina, electoral law established a 30 per cent quota for candidates. Quotas may also be symbolic of a desired modern and democratic, but contested and uncertain, future. In South Africa, women (mainly ANC women) pushed for quotas and a substantial presence in the legislature, yet women workers have been raped in the Parliament building (Dahlerup 2002). Quotas do not guarantee increases in women's political representation. Krook (2003) shows that quotas are present in political systems with high, medium and low levels of women's political representation. The 30 per cent quotas in Bolivia and Brazil, for example, have so far led to representations of women in national legislatures of 19 and 12 per cent respectively. The parity law, a 50 per cent quota, led to little change in the presence of women in the French National Assembly and to disappointing results in local elections (see chapter 5). It may be that quotas take time and their implementation involves policy learning. For example, in Belgium, disappointing results in the first parity elections led to rule changes and the expansion of sanctions to improve the results of the next round (Meier 2005).

Male party leaders agree to the implementation of quotas for mainly strategic reasons. However, debates are shaped by particular traditions. Parties of the left have traditions of equality that make them more likely to support claims for equality, which may make it easier for women's advocates to form internal coalitions for change. Although support for quotas to increase women's representation is less likely on the right, there are many examples of right-wing support. Italy, where politicians from the extreme right, notably the Fascist Alessandra Mussolini, have advocated quotas is a contemporary example (Guadagnini 2005).

Pragmatic considerations are important in decisions by male-dominated parties to introduce quotas. They may wish to make a claim that they represent women and require quotas as a symbolic means of demonstrating their commitment to meeting that obligation. They may be responding to the claims of party members who have come to see the importance of quotas if change is to occur (Guadagnini 2005). Carlos Mennen supported quotas when he thought he would lose an election if he did not. Many Eastern European regimes, having rejected quotas in the early stages of democratization, later returned to them in part because alliances with Western European countries made it politically attractive to meet claims for women's representation. Such 'contagion effects' in modern democracies are most likely to be found in proportional systems (Matland and Studlar 1996).

Above all, quotas are political strategies. They do not come into being by accident and they do not guarantee the election of feminist politicians, as the fortunes of Front National women in France vividly demonstrate. The distinction between incremental and fast-track quotas illuminates the impact of different institutional, historical and cultural contexts, all of which affect whether quotas are adopted, what kind of quota is used and how effectively they are implemented.

Whatever the context, however, women's agency is critical to decisions to adopt quotas. The achievement of increased women's political representation rarely takes place without a political struggle in which equality advocates must both mobilize and take advantage of the available opportunities. Party women's organizations, feminist movements and women's interest groups have become skilled at demanding quotas to achieve increases in women's political representation. To illustrate this argument, and to show how quotas work in practice, in the next chapter I describe two movements for quotas: the all-women shortlists campaigns in the British Labour Party and the *parité* movement in France.

5

Examples: Quotas and Parité

Why Britain and France?

Britain and France are contrasting examples of the movement for and implementation of quotas. The have much in common but also are different in important ways. At national level their different majoritarian systems are inhospitable to women. In both countries, quota movements took off in the 1990s when their representation of women in the legislatures were amongst the lowest in Europe. In both countries the debates resulted in the adoption of quotas. But the quotas adopted were of different types. While in Britain they remained mainly an internal party matter, in France they involved constitutional changes and alterations to electoral law that at municipal and department level compelled parties to nominate women. In both, implementation has been a problem at national levels of office and less of a problem at lower levels. This is partly because below national level, both countries offer proportional electoral systems. In both, the key decisions are made by political parties, and in both, quota advocates mobilized inside and outside the political parties. Between them, they illustrate well the politics of adopting and using quotas in difficult political systems.

The British Example

The British example illustrates the interplay of agency, institutions and opportunities in decisions to use quotas. Many of the characteristic features of quota politics, including the importance of electoral systems and political parties, the opportunities offered by party modernization, system change and the contextualized, protracted and contingent nature of the process, are evident in this example.

In the past Britain has been a particularly difficult system to feminize. However, institutional opportunities have recently changed. In the wake of a wave of constitutional change we can find illustrations of many electoral settings in mainland Britain. Elections to the House of Commons take place through single member simple majority constituency-based systems. For the European Parliament the method is the closed party list system. For the Scottish Parliament and Welsh Assembly, election is via an additional member system combining first-past-the-post constituencies with party lists. For the Greater London Authority, election is by the additional member system.

The different electoral systems for different kinds of assembly offer opportunities for different methods of quotas. In proportional systems, where closed party lists are presented to voters who must vote for or against the list in the order in which it is presented, parties can ensure the election of women by placing them in high positions on the lists. In constituency elections where only one representative may be returned, the placement of women is more conspicuous and even more controversial, and hence may involve more pressure on local selectors.

In Britain a division of labour on issues of women's political representation between autonomous women's organizations and party feminists characterizes the quota movements. The contribution of autonomous feminists is possible because independent, that is non-partisan, advocacy organizations can make public criticisms that party feminists are prevented from making because of expectations of party loyalty. However, feminists mobilized inside the political parties are crucial. Historically, the Labour Party has made most use of quotas of candidates, but most other mainland parties have adopted internal quotas of one kind or another. Internal quotas are aimed at party positions such as branch officers and executive committee memberships.

The process of change that took place in the Labour Party is instructive. It shows the importance of institutional culture, opportunity and the detail of particular mechanisms in explanations for the adoption and effectiveness of quotas. From 1979, successive debates in the Labour Party about women's roles included claims for equal political representation. The earlier debates were set in a changing context of fierce internal arguments about party modernization strategies following each of four successive electoral defeats. The later debates took place after Labour's landslide election victory in 1997 when the context again changed significantly. The modernization debates were about party organization and policy. Hence, the feminization debates addressed both internal organizational and policy matters. Organizational issues included leadership selection, candidate selection, the role of members, the role of the party conference and the National Executive Committee (NEC), the roles of the trade unions and the appropriate mechanisms for policy formation.

Throughout this period there were changes to methods of candidate selection within the Labour Party. There were procedural changes in which successive proposals to enhance women's selection opportunities were made. The surrounding debates provided opportunities to raise questions about women's roles, including issues of presence such as their representation in the party and in the legislature and substantive policy issues such as childcare, equal pay, equal opportunities, domestic violence, etc. Presence issues were also addressed in policy debates, notably after the party's defeat in the 1983 general election when party women complained that they were excluded from the post-mortem policy discussions.

To understand these debates, it is necessary both to describe the wider party conflict in which they were set and to describe internal party women's policy machinery and networks present at the time. During the years of the debates the women's policy network in the Labour Party changed significantly. From an almost dormant arrangement that included a women's conference and women's sections, serviced by a women's officer, it grew to cover various internal offices, committees and sections, as well as internal advocacy organizations in the form of campaigns, networks or factions.

There have been feminists in the British Labour Party since it was first established. Women's sections were created in the 1918 party constitution. But they institutionalized separate spheres and tended to cut most women off from the main party organization. Furthermore, they had no direct powers of decision-making and no direct representation on party decision-making bodies (Perrigo 1996: 121). Their limited influence waned after the Second World War and, by the 1960s, women's voices were not much heard. When the second wave of feminism emerged at the end of the decade, it appeared to many participants that Labour was not a fruitful arena for feminist politics. But, after the election of Margaret Thatcher's Conservative government in 1979, feminists joined the party in increasing numbers. At the same time feminists who were already party members became more vocal and other women in the party became more feminist (Lovenduski and Randall 1993).

The modernization process in the party gave feminists repeated opportunities to organize and to press claims for women throughout the 1980s and 1990s. It is important to understand how inhospitable the ethos of the party was to women whose political experience was mainly gained in the new social movement activities of the 1970s. In the areas of Britain where Labour is strongest, the dominant ethos was, and in some areas still is, informed by the patriarchal culture of the traditional unions. Although those unions were in decline, they left a residue of elaborate, ritualized, formalized, hierarchical politics. To be effective, individuals had to be familiar with the 'rule book' that set out the terms of party organization and spelled out procedure. A second barrier was the culture of the trade unions, which operated a sort of cordon sanitaire of sexism around the party. Until quite recently, political effectiveness in the Labour Party also required a base in a trade union. Trade unions largely operated along similar lines to the Labour Party in that they were rule-book driven and did not welcome any intervention by women. Even under New Labour a union base is an advantage for aspirant candidates. A long political apprenticeship was necessary for individuals to learn the rules and to be able to use them effectively. The party culture was a barrier to the exercise of influence by all new members and it proved especially unpleasant for incoming women who often had little other organizational experience.

After 1979 women began to challenge that culture by intervening in the post-election debates. Important policy decisions can be identified in six different periods, mainly corresponding to the Westminster electoral cycle. Labour's four electoral defeats of 1979, 1983, 1987 and 1992, and their consequent diagnosis and succeeding policy reviews, opened a series of modernization debates within the party. Of these, the most important in system terms were the debates on party structure and candidate selection. Following victories in 1997 and 2001, the party revisited the issue in discussion of candidate selection mechanisms for various levels of election.

1979–1983: Conflict

Ideological polarization between the parliamentary party and key trade unions set in after the 1979 electoral defeat, leading to the 1981 Wembley Conference at which changes in leadership selection methods drove prominent leading members to establish a new party, the Social Democratic Party (SDP). The Wembley Conference and its consequences marked a shift to the left by Labour and opened a period of considerable internal turmoil. The shift to the left attracted socialist feminists into the party. Alarmed by policies of the Thatcher government, many feminists who previously had not engaged in institutional politics now felt they should. The crisis in the party opened up spaces for them (Perrigo 1996: 120–1).

The first sign of their impact was the new vitality of the internal party women's organization, which became a focus for incoming feminists who developed both its networking and policy formulation activities. The effects were first seen in the draft programme, 'Labour's Programme 1982'. The document contained a number of pledges aimed directly at women, many of which appeared in the 1983 Labour Election Manifesto (Perrigo).

Although policies directed at women's interests were adopted, demands for the political representation of women did not get much purchase. Perrigo (1996) argues that, despite apparent opportunities created by organizational reform, women were actually disadvantaged by its implementation. Mandatory reselection of sitting MPs by their constituency party, adopted after 1979, for example, should have increased turnover and brought in more women. However, there were only eight reselections between 1979 and 1983 and only one brought in a woman – a very important woman to later developments – Clare Short. The other major reform of that period, the altered system of election to party leadership, did nothing for women. The reform strengthened the power of trade unions, which were opposed to the demands of women at that time.

1983–1987: Party modernization – one woman on a shortlist

The disastrous defeat in the 1983 general election opened the way to sweeping reform. It was a devastating defeat for

Labour, which almost slipped into third place in terms of share of the total votes cast. This defeat discredited the party left wing and began the modernization process that continues until the present time. The reforms initiated by Neil Kinnock after 1983 were designed to appeal to voters and to make the party more attractive to individual members by giving them more power. Kinnock's aim was to defeat the 'hard left' of the party, a project in which he largely succeeded. But full modernization and democratization required shifting the power of the traditional unions. As the 'hard left' declined, attention turned to the party–union relationship, which was increasingly seen as an electoral liability.

During these years, unions, particularly the traditional manufacturing and extractive industry unions, declined both in numbers and as political forces, the victims, variously, of unemployment, de-industrialization, demographic change and Thatcherism. New forms of employment were part-time, service-sector jobs mainly taken by women, who accounted for virtually all of new union membership during the 1980s. At the same time, women were becoming more active in their trade unions. They were especially active in the white-collar and service unions, which became more important in the union movement as they displaced the more patriarchal and authoritarian traditional unions in the declining manufacturing and extractive industries. Thus the 1980s were a time of increased opportunities for feminists in the party. Not only did they gain vital political experience and credentials, they also benefited from shifts in the rules that allowed feminist interventions.

In the wake of electoral defeat came changes in the party that forced the leadership to attend to women members. The newly formed, breakaway SDP opened a competition for women's votes by introducing a women's quota at the shortlisting stage of their selection process for parliamentary candidates. This is another example of how the creation of a new institution, in this case a political party, increased opportunities to claim women's representation. The SDP purported to be an open modern party, responsive to constituencies long ignored by Labour.

Labour began to pay more attention to its women members and constituents. Claims for the increased representation of women became more effective. The first 'quota' was adopted for the 1987 general election when a system was adopted that required the compulsory shortlisting of a woman in any selecting constituency to which at least one woman applied. In 1984 Labour's NEC appointed Jo Richardson MP as Shadow Spokesperson for Women, and issued a charter for equality for women in the party. The charter urged all sections to appoint women's officers and examine their procedures to see if they discriminated against women. In short, the charter urged positive action but did not require it. This was classic equality rhetoric, but as is so often the case with rhetorical action in politics, it led to more effective measures. The hare had been set running.

Women's mobilization in the party increased throughout the period. A left-wing feminist group, Labour Women's Action Committee (LWAC), developed an effective campaigning strategy, widening and deepening debate about women in the party. Although the 1983 election returned only ten Labour women, these included Harriet Harman (first elected in 1982) and Clare Short, who were sympathetic to women's claims and who pressed women's concerns about representation. Women began to win more support in the trade unions, which were experiencing their own crises of role and recruitment and were increasingly responsive to the demands of women (Perrigo 1996: 125). For example, the Trades Union Congress (TUC) established an Equal Rights Unit in the early 1980s. Trade union women activists also tended to be active in the Labour Party, hence 'doubling' the effect of their efforts. Support for the possibility of a Ministry for Women gained ground around this time. The proposal came from Jo Richardson in 1986 in a party discussion document entitled 'Labour's Ministry for Women's Rights'. The proposal was endorsed by the NEC in 1987.

1987–1992: Internal party quotas

Labour's third successive electoral defeat occurred in 1987 and was followed by the usual policy review. The part played in the party by the trade unions and candidate selection continued to be crucial organizational issues. A change in party campaigning strategy resulted in greater attention being paid to public opinion research that led in turn to more attention to women voters. In a by now familiar oversight, the policy review after the defeat produced a number of commitments to women but was heavily criticized because women in the party were excluded from the discussion. In response, Jo Richardson set up and chaired a women's monitoring committee to ensure that their progress in the party was recorded and that women's concerns were fed into the party's policy process. Women were included in the drafting of the 1990 party publication, 'Looking to the Future', which spelled out in detail proposals for the Ministry for Women, promising that it would have cabinet status in a Labour government.

During this period, following pressure from the Women's Committee on the NEC, the decision was taken to strengthen women's equality machinery in the party organization by upgrading the post of women's officer to a senior position. Crucial to the process was the support of the trade unions, which had become more women-friendly in response to internal campaigns as well as to continued labour market change. Within the party, women became increasingly mobilized. A group called Labour Women's Network (LWN) concentrated on getting more women into elected office. LWN produced pamphlets, organized votes, generated debates and trained aspirant women candidates. A 1990 Fabian pamphlet by Rachel Brooks, Angela Eagle and Clare Short called for compulsory quotas throughout the party, including all-women shortlists for parliamentary selection. The 1990 annual conference approved the implementation of many of their proposals, agreeing that internal quotas should be set to ensure that women would make up 40 per cent of any body involved in the party decision-making machinery and calling on the NEC to bring forward proposals to achieve this. The same conference agreed to quotas throughout all the party organizations, including branch and constituency committees, NEC and annual conference delegations, and a quota of women was introduced into shadow cabinet elections.

The radical rule was that if a woman was not found for a quota position, that position remained vacant. This conference also set a time limit, of three general elections, to bring the proportion of women in the Parliamentary Labour Party (PLP) up to 50 per cent, but no means to achieve the target was established.

In 1991, rule changes were passed by the annual conference to implement internal party quotas. These included a 40 per cent quota for women on the NEC, to be phased in by 1995. There would be a quota of conference delegates that ensured that local parties sent equal numbers of men and women to national and regional conferences. Within local parties, quotas would ensure that roughly half the officers at branch and constituency level were women. Internal quotas were taken seriously and implemented, not least because of the assiduous work of Deborah Lincoln, who became the Labour Party Women's Officer in 1988. Gradually, Lincoln and Clare Short, who was on the NEC Women's Committee, became convinced that equality of women's parliamentary representation required compulsory quotas of some kind. They were supported by women throughout the party. They also had powerful male allies. Larry Whitty and Peter Coleman supported them from within the organization. At that time, they were senior party officials, and they became convinced that quotas would be necessary in the course of their efforts to persuade constituencies to select more women. Luminaries such as Gordon Brown and John Prescott were also supportive of increased women's representation at that time.

1992–1997: All-women shortlists

In 1992 Labour lost its fourth successive general election. Polling indicated that a gender gap, whereby women were less likely to vote Labour than men, had reopened after apparently closing in 1987. Internal analyses of the polls revealed that had women voted Labour in the same proportions as men, Labour would have won the election. Taking responsibility for defeat, Kinnock resigned and was succeeded by John Smith, who proved particularly sympathetic to demands for women's representation. Clare Short became Shadow Minister for Women and Chair of the NEC Women's Committee. Her tenure in these two posts marked a significant period of progress for women.

In 1992 the party introduced internal discussion forums for developing policy. None had special responsibility for women, but each had a brief to consider the implications of policy for women. The policy forums were set up after the party had agreed to the implementation of quotas for women of 40 per cent throughout the organization; as a result 40 per cent of the delegates at the policy forums were women (Perrigo 1996: 125). Support for quotas grew and internal feminist capacity increased, a development illustrated by the growing activity of internal women's organizations. After 1992 LWAC supported a demand for more women MPs, dropping the divisive condition that the women's organization itself be represented. LWN became more influential and a group called EMILY was founded in 1992 by Barbara Follett and others to finance women's candidacies.

Support for equality guarantees grew. The chosen mechanism was specific to party candidate selection conventions. Advocates campaigned for the adoption of all-women shortlists (AWS), an arrangement whereby selectors in some constituencies would choose their candidates from shortlists of women: there would be a choice of women, but men would not be eligible to stand in those constituencies. In 1993 the annual party conference agreed to the introduction of AWS. It did so in the context of debate over changes in candidate selection procedures, another example of how the modernization debate opened up space for women's representation advocates to insert them into debates. The mechanism was part of the package of parliamentary selection reform, which included the move to a one member one vote system (OMOV). The vote was extremely close and passed only because one union, the Manufacturing, Science and Finance Union (MSF), so strongly supported an increase of women's representation that it abstained, despite being opposed to OMOV. MSF explicitly made the decision to abstain on the grounds that it did not want its opposition to OMOV to prevent the adoption of AWS.

How did the deal get done? Essentially it was a product of what had gone before. The first step on this route was the 'one woman on a shortlist' rule adopted in 1988. The Labour Party took the next in 1989 when, following a proposal from the Tribune Group (an internal left-wing faction), a quota was introduced in the shadow cabinet. The quota required all MPs to cast votes for three women in order for their ballot paper to be valid. The size of the shadow cabinet was increased by three from a membership of 15 to one of 18 so that no male 'losers' were created by the new policy.

Response to the policy of internal quotas varied. There was great support in many parts of the party but considerable opposition in some traditional Labour areas. Nevertheless, the forward march of women continued. The significant exception to a widespread initial acceptance of quotas was in the case of the selection of parliamentary candidates. On this matter policy remained weak. There was no compulsion to select women, only to shortlist one of them and then only in seats to which a woman applied. There was no requirement for constituency parties to seek out and recruit potential women candidates.

More women were selected throughout the 1979–92 period, but, as table 5.1 shows, while the number of women

Examples: Quotas and Parité

Table 5.1 Labour women MPs and candidates, 1979–1992

	PPCs	MPs	Success rate
1979	52	11	21.2
1983	78	10	12.8
1987	92	21	22.8
1992	138	37	26.8

nominated increased at every election, most nominations were in unwinnable or marginal seats. In 1992 Labour returned only 37 women, 14 per cent of the Parliamentary Labour Party, despite fielding 138 women candidates. Of the 20 Labour MPs who retired in safe seats that year, 18 were replaced by men.

Without some mechanism to secure improvement, progress in women's representation was barely perceptible. But designing a suitable mechanism proved difficult. The system was and is characterized by low incumbency turnover and the predominance of safe seats. It awards a huge advantage to incumbent MPs. At each election only a few retirements take place and only a few vacancies occur. Most of the turnover occurs in marginal seats, a few of which change hands at each election. By contrast to the list systems of many other democracies, the system of elections to the House of Commons offered no simple means of making rapid improvements in the proportion of women MPs. In this winner-takes-all system each selection for a winnable or vacant seat was perceived as a 'zero sum game' in which insiders – normally men – had the advantage. It became increasingly clear that local selectors, who had the major say in candidate selection, were favouring 'typical' male candidates and effectively blocking good women from taking winnable seats. This impression was confirmed by academic research. The 1992 British Candidate Study, for example (Norris and Lovenduski 1995), found Labour selectors to be resistant to women candidates.

Many observers were surprised when Labour adopted its AWS policy. However, the idea had a long history. For many years the Labour Party women's conference voted for AWS as a requirement in all seats which Labour was likely to win with a small electoral swing or where Labour MPs were retiring. These proposals were repeatedly voted down at the annual conference.

In the early 1990s a compromise was found. The compromise was managed by Clare Short in her role as chair of the NEC Women's Committee, working with the party general secretary Larry Whitty, senior party staff and women in the party. They proposed to apply AWS in half of all winnable seats. The AWS seats would be selected by regional consultations attended by officers from all constituency parties. The mechanism offered a breakthrough. Within each of the party's regions the policy applied both to seats where Labour MPs retired and to target marginals. Because it allowed men access to half of the new seats that became available, ensuring that popular male candidates who had fought seats previously were protected, the decision was felt to be fair. Because it included constituency parties in the process of deciding which seats were to use AWS, it was thought to be workable. By the time it came to be approved at the annual conference, all-women shortlists had the support of many members who, although long-standing advocates of women's equality, had previously opposed compulsory quotas. Their support came after years of trying weaker equality promotion measures that delivered only small increases in women's presence. Only after other avenues had been thoroughly explored did they conclude that there was no alternative.

Although falling far short of the radical position sought by the women's conference, the policy was still controversial. It was won only with the full backing of John Smith, then leader of the party. After consultation, an 'options' paper was put to the NEC Women's Committee, at a meeting that he made a point of attending. He gave his commitment to ensuring that the chosen option of AWS in half of all winnable seats was supported by the annual conference. In 1993, as described above, conference supported the proposal in one of the most hard-fought debates of recent years.

Having agreed the measure, the party addressed the issue of how to implement it. The means of deciding which half of the seats should have all-women shortlists was critical and extremely sensitive. The shortlists were to apply in half the 'safe' Labour seats where MPs retired and also in half the target marginal seats. It was important that women were not left with the least winnable of the latter. The method chosen was to require half the seats in each region to adopt AWS, with the decision on seats to be sought by consensus at regional level meetings of officers from all the constituencies concerned. Crucial to implementation was the earlier decision to require half the constituency officers to be women, which meant that consensus meetings were attended by many supporters of the policy.

Leadership support was also crucial. After John Smith died in 1993, he was replaced by Tony Blair, who was less sympathetic to the use of quotas. Blair's election marked the imposition of increased leader control of the party, a process defended in terms of the need to make Labour electable. AWS got a bad press and were seen as damaging to the party. However, at the 1994 annual conference the policy was again the subject of debate. Blair, who had previously publicly declared his unhappiness with it, did not take a position in the debate. Clare Short and Deborah Lincoln, supported by Anne Gibson of MSF (who had brokered the OMOV/AWS deal in 1993) and other activists, led the debate and the policy was retained.

As plans for implementation progressed, the controversy continued. There was hostility from many men in the party, with some – including Members of Parliament – taking up the frequent opportunities offered by the press to 'rubbish' the policy. Ann Carlton, an activist in the Welsh party, set up the campaign group 'Labour Supporters for Real Equality', which was a small group but received considerable press attention. The *Daily Mail*, in particular, did as much as it could to fan the flames. For example, the paper ran a regular column reporting and criticizing quota selections. There were problems in reaching a consensus in the party's north-west region. In the south, the Slough constituency was forced by the NEC to accept an all-women shortlist when the local party failed to agree. Nevertheless, by January 1996 consensus meetings had been held in all regions and most parliamentary candidates in key target seats were in place. One-half of them (33) were women chosen from all-women shortlists. In addition, two women were selected in this way to replace retiring Labour MPs in 'safe' seats.

However, the mechanism was brought to an abrupt end when two disgruntled male aspirants took the party to court. On 8 January 1996 the Leeds Industrial Tribunal (Jepson and Dyas-Elliott v. The Labour Party and Others) declared that selection procedures of political parties (normally exempt from the provisions of the sex discrimination legislation) facilitate access to employment and that AWS contravened the Sex Discrimination Act. Anxious to complete its selections in good time for the general election and concerned not to jeopardize the positions of women already selected under the policy, the NEC decided not to appeal the decision. Instead, a working party was established to identify effective and legal ways to maximize the number of women candidates nominated and selected in the remaining vacant Labour seats. Very few women were selected after the tribunal decision. The Leeds industrial tribunal changed the landscape by ruling that the role of a parliamentary candidate could be considered as employment for the purposes of the Sex Discrimination Act. The judgement disregarded the fact that political parties are explicitly exempted from the scope of the Act, and that, legally, the means of becoming an MP was, and is, in the hands of the electorate and not the party. In broad terms, the implications of the Leeds decision were that any selection procedure undertaken by a political party for elected and salaried office could be subject to complaint if equal opportunities procedures were not followed (Russell 2000).

Although controversial, all-women shortlists were highly successful. The real effect of the policy was not so much that it led to an increase in the number of women candidates – they had been increasing steadily for the last five elections – but that women were selected for winnable seats. Thus in 1997, Labour women candidates increased their success rates to a dramatic 64 per cent as 101 of 158 women candidates were elected. Women constituted 24.6 per cent of candidates and 24.1 per cent of elected Labour MPs (Eagle and Lovenduski 1998).

1997–2001: Quotas for devolution, but 50/50 shortlists for Westminster

After victory (and immediately before, see above), candidate selection mechanisms came under review once again, not only for Westminster but also for the soon to be established Scottish Parliament, Welsh Assembly and London Assembly, for local government and the European Parliament. To address the selection of women candidates for the new elections and in the changed circumstances at Westminster, Hilary Armstrong MP (chair of the NEC Women's Committee from 1996 to 1997) chaired an internal Women's Representation Taskforce. The taskforce met during the winter and spring of 1996–7. Its members included the women's officer, delegates and party officials from Scotland and Wales and experts. It reviewed mechanisms for selection and made recommendations to the candidates' office of the party. The Scotland and Wales mechanisms became part of a legal debate within the government. However, quotas of women candidates for Westminster were explicitly ruled out. The working party recommended 50/50 shortlists for women and men as the least bad option. The new rules were adopted in the context of a major internal debate in the party over the discussion document 'Party into Power', which was a proposal to restructure the party giving more power to individual members, and further revising the party relationship with the trade unions. Once again, candidate selection was under review.

Elections in Scotland and Wales took place under the additional member system whereby traditional plurality constituency seats were topped up by party list seats set aside for the purpose of ensuring proportionality of party seats and votes. The constituencies were based on the European parliamentary electoral constituencies; hence parties had a fair idea of where and how they were likely to win seats. In this system different strategies were available to different parties depending upon their electoral position. It is a convention in the study of women and politics that list systems offer parties better chances of improving women's representation because they encourage the presentation of socially balanced slates of candidates. However, Labour knew that in Scotland and Wales its successes would come in constituency seats. So, as at Westminster, a device had to be found that would assure election of women in a single member plurality vote contest.

The industrial tribunal decision and the surrounding legal confusion probably explain Labour's hesitation over Westminster selections. In Scotland and Wales, however, Labour was persuaded that a system of 'twinning' of constituencies to stand male and female candidates jointly was legally feasible. It was also politically feasible. Aspirant candidates for the new legislatures were, for the first time, subjected to formal vetting. They were required first to seek approval by applying for inclusion on a panel of acceptable candidates. Constituencies were then required to select from that panel. In terms of legal procedure, only candidates accepted by the party would be in a position to make a legal complaint. However, those who were approved for panels were unlikely to take the party to a tribunal for breach of employment rights. The twinning mechanism operated as follows. Constituencies were matched according to proximity and winnability. Both women and men applied. Each constituency drew up a balanced shortlist of women and men. Then, the shortlists were merged and constituency members voted. The top ranked women and men were selected (Russell et al. 2002).

The decision to implement quotas in the form of twinning in Scotland and Wales was an indication that, despite the risk of legal challenge, Labour was committed to the equal representation of women in the new institutions. The decision was a watershed. Since the first Scottish and Welsh elections, Labour has repeatedly implemented quotas.

Why? Meg Russell (2003) argues there were at least four reasons for the decision. First, the symbolic effect of women's success in the 1997 general election was thought to be an asset for the party, leading to an important connection between the presence of women and political modernization. Moreover, the Conservatives were opposed to devolution and argued that it was yet another means for the usual local government suspects to win lucrative positions for themselves. The nomination of women, who were not the usual suspects, undermined this criticism. Second, Labour was publicly committed to field equal numbers of women and men candidates in Scotland, a commitment that, third, women's advocates insisted, and Labour leaders agreed, should extend to Wales and the new London Assembly. Fourth, internal party quotas and the increase of women MPs after 1997 placed a number of women supporters of quotas in powerful positions from where they could their influence to introduce the measures.

Two further points should be added to Russell's argument. First, patterns of electoral competition in Scotland and Wales differed from those for Westminster elections. Nationalist and Liberal Democratic parties were strong in both countries. They were expected to benefit from the more proportional electoral systems of the new assemblies. Second, the implementation of quotas strengthened the arguments for launching a more professional system of candidate recruitment in Scotland and Wales. The system allowed selectors to choose a new kind of candidate, better suited to New

Labour aspirations and images. Labour's decision put pressure on other parties in the post-devolution elections and, when most of them failed to deliver as good a proportion of women candidates in winnable seats, exposed their weak commitment to equality of representation.

Predictably, the Conservatives did not provide for the selection of women candidates in the devolution elections. Liberal Democrats in Scotland operated gender-balanced shortlists but made no provision for women actually to be selected. They rejected proposals for zipping or for placing women first on their regional lists, and in Scotland they elected only two women. The Scottish National Party (SNP) did not apply a quota in Scotland, but 43 per cent of their candidates elected to the Scottish Parliament were women. In 1999 the SNP was Labour's main competitor in Scotland. The SNP was formally committed to women's political representation but opposed to quotas. Although the party debated various quota mechanisms in the run-up to the elections, they were not adopted. However, after considerable encouragement from the leadership, selecting committees in the regions placed women high on their lists.

In Wales, support for women's representation was weaker and women's advocates were less well organized. Nevertheless, Labour adopted twinning there too, against considerable opposition from local party leaders. As in Scotland, twinning was important to Labour plans because the party had a low expectation of winning any list seats, so the placement of women on lists offered no realistic hope of topping up their representation if the constituency seats did not deliver. In contrast to the SNP, Plaid Cymru formally operated a gender template whereby the first and third place on each of five regional party lists were women. Liberal Democrats stopped short of quotas but actively encouraged women to be candidates who were mainly selected or placed in seats that party strategists believed were marginal. Because both the Liberal Democrats and Plaid Cymru won more seats than they expected, their women candidates did well.

Table 5.2   Women and men elected to the Scottish Parliament 1999, by party and type of seat

Party	Constituency seats		List seats		Total	
	Men	Women	Men	Women	Seats	% Women
Labour	27	26	1	2	56	50
SNP	5	2	15	13	35	43
Conservative	0	0	15	3	18	17
Lib Dem	10	2	5	0	17	12
Green	0	0	1	0	1	0
Scottish Socialist	0	0	1	0	1	0
Independent	1	0	0	0	1	0
Total	44	29	38	18	129	37

Source: Adapted from Mackay 2003

Table 5.3   Women and men elected to the Welsh Assembly 1999, by party and type of seat

Party	Constituency seats		List seats		Total	
	Men	Women	Men	Women	Seats	% Women
Labour	12	15	1	0	28	54
Plaid Cymru	7	2	4	4	17	29
Conservative	1	0	8	0	9	0
Lib Dem	1	2	2	1	6	50
Total	21	19	15	5	60	40

Source: Adapted from Mackay 2003

The results of the first devolution elections were unprecedented in British politics. In Scotland, 37 per cent of MSPs (Members of the Scottish Parliament) were women and in Wales 40 per cent of AMs (Assembly Members) were women. But, as tables 5.2 and 5.3 show, the increase was the product of the work of a limited number of parties. This breakthrough in 1999 was widely hailed by women's advocates. It marked a sharp turn in the British quota debates. The success of women led to a rerun of all the quota arguments and un- doubtedly affected opinion about special measures to ensure women's representation. For a while it seemed that the case for quotas was won. Shortly thereafter, in 2000, in elections to the new London Assembly, Labour used twinning for its candidate selection and the Greater London Authority (GLA) was elected with 40 per cent women. In the same year the Wakeham Commission reported its proposals on the reform of the House of Lords and recommended a quota of 30 per cent women amongst appointees.

2001– : The Sex Discrimination Electoral Candidates Act

The quota debates in Britain have been characterized by continuous change. Quotas were first accepted in principle by the Labour Party in 1988, an acceptance made explicit in succeeding years. The intervening years of living with the policy of quotas on internal positions affected both the cul- ture and decision-making in the party. In 1996 the illegality of quotas for electoral candidates was asserted in the Jepson v. Dyas Eliot industrial tribunal decision. This decision, at first considered doubtful, was thought to be confirmed by the Sawyer v. Ashan case in 1999. This case involved an Employ- ment Appeal Tribunal brought under the Race Relations Act of 1976. The Tribunal confirmed that candidate selection was subject to employment discrimination legislation (Russell 2000). These cases set a new context in which parties needed to consider the possible legal implications of any action under employment law.

Despite implementing quotas for elections to the devolved assemblies, Labour was unwilling to take the arguably greater legal risks of implementing candidate quotas for Westmin- ster. As the 2001 general election approached, amid frequent predictions of a fall in the number of Labour women MPs, party equality advocates mobilized for a reinstatement of all-women shortlists. Many argued that the Amsterdam Treaty, signed in 1997, permitted equality guarantees. An influential report by Meg Russell (2000) assembled legal opinion that such measures were congruent with EU law. By the time the 2001 election took place, the government was persuaded that a change in the law was necessary. Equality advocates and women MPs kept up the pressure. Fawcett published an influential report on discrimination against well-qualified women candidates that was widely reported in the press (Shepherd-Robinson and Lovenduski 2001). The campaign was assisted by the brief tenure of Baroness Sally Morgan, a trusted Blair adviser, as Minister for Women. Morgan had been a supporter of women's representation for many years. In the aftermath of the industrial tribunal decisions she became convinced that the AWS policy was necessary.

The government honoured its commitment and the Sex Discrimination Election Candidates Bill received royal assent in 2002. It was a permissive measure that allowed parties to adopt quotas but did not require them to do so. The measure passed against little opposition. All but a few opponents stayed away from the debate – i.e. abstained from voting. The Act contained an unusual sunset clause ending in 2015. The temporary nature of the policy was agreed in order to ensure compliance with European law.

Although the argument for quotas appeared to be won in the Labour Party by 2001, within the other parties opposition grew. At their 2001 conference Liberal Democrats failed to adopt quotas, as opponents mounted fierce and effective opposition. Young Liberal women wearing pink t-shirts bearing the slogan 'I am not a token woman' symbolized the opposition to the proposals. In 2002 the t-shirts reappeared and the Liberal Democratic Party conference voted to go back on its previously successful experiment with 'zipping' in European elections. Previously, in the 1999 European elections, Liberal Democrats had placed women and men in alternate positions on party lists, electing five men and five women to the European Parliament. The 2002 conference decided that there would be only one woman of three on the list in the 2004 European parliamentary elections. Conservatives too opposed the adoption of quotas. Their public rhetoric was that they preferred to persuade constituencies to adopt women in winnable seats. When appointed party chairman in 2002, Teresa May quietly dropped her advocacy of gender-balanced shortlists.

In 2003 new elections for the Scottish Parliament and the Welsh Assembly were held. At both Holyrood and Cardiff Bay the share of seats won by women increased. In Scotland the number of women rose from 48 to 52. Both the Labour Party and the Scottish Socialist Party operated quotas of women in their selection process. Both increased their proportions of women MSPs. The Greens also increased their proportion of women, but without the use of quotas. In Wales women won 30 of the 60 Assembly seats. The Welsh Labour Party and Plaid Cymru used quotas, while the Welsh Liberal Democrats relied on encouraging their women members to stand. Labour, Plaid Cymru and the Conservatives increased their percentages of elected women and the Liberal Democrats maintained their 50/50 balance.

Table 5.4 illustrates the variations in women's political representation in British political parties at different levels of election. The table offers very little support for the prospect of equality of women's representation without the use of quotas. For example, the proportion of nationalist women MSPs fell in 2003, when the SNP vote collapsed. Even without party incumbents, Conservatives were unable to produce a substantial presence of women in their Welsh and Scottish delegations (although it was better than at Westminster). Only two fairly small parties, the Welsh Liberal Democrats and Scottish Greens, managed an equal number of women and men representatives without quotas.

Table 5.4 indicates that progress is being made in the political parties, but where there are no quotas it tends to be

Table 5.4   Women's representation as a percentage of party representation in UK political institutions, 2003

Party	Conservative	Labour	LibDem	SNP	PC	Other	% of total
House of Commons	8	23	10	20	–	17	18
House of Lords	15	22	23	–	–	10	16
Welsh Assembly 2003	18	*54*	50	NA	50	–	50
Scottish Parliament 2003	22	*56*	12	33	NA	47	40
Northern Ireland Assembly						14	14
European Parliament UK Members	8	33	*45*	–	50	33	24
Local Authorities England and Wales	26	26	34	–	15	22	27

Note: Numbers in italics indicate the use of quotas of women candidates

slow. In Britain the quota debate continues as attention is drawn not only to the failures of major parties to nominate women for winnable seats, but also to the representation of women in the devolved assemblies, regional government, in local government and in the European Parliament. That women representatives will increase votes for the party is part of the argument. The ongoing debate means the issue stays on the agenda, but it also keeps expectations of women politicians high.

In the British system of party government, changes in party selection practices are the key to increasing the number of women representatives. Debates have taken place in all the major parties. In the Labour Party, quotas of women are now an established part of the party culture, at least as far as internal party positions are concerned. Labour selection policy is at its strongest in the selection of candidates for local elections. In 2004 incumbent men were replaced by women candidates where that was necessary to meet the party target of one-third women councillors. In the course of the various debates, the rights of women voters to be represented by women and the rights of women to be nominated were explicitly asserted. Within the Labour Party, discussion of quotas ranged across substantive policy issues, the necessity for the party to present a women-friendly image and the need for women to be represented by women. Claims were made that increasing women's representation would improve the appeal of the party to voters and the party's ability to make policies that incorporate women's interests and perspectives (Childs 2004a; MacDougal 1997; Short 1996). These debates are now being repeated in the Conservative and Liberal Democratic parties where candidate selection systems are recognized to be barriers to women and appropriate means to overcome selection obstacles to women are sought. The issue of quotas has also been revisited in the SNP. As the party's electoral fortunes have declined, attention was drawn to the fall in the number of its women MSPs from 50 to 33 per cent in 2003 and the presence of only one woman in its Westminster delegation. During 2004, SNP leaders raised the issue of quotas in discussions of internal reform designed to revitalize the party that are reminiscent of the Labour modernization debates of the 1980s and early 1990s (*Edinburgh Evening News*, 23 July 2004; *The Scotsman*, 26 January 2004).

France

The French example of quota legislation offers an interesting contrasting example. France is one of only two Western European countries to adopt a system of legislative quotas. As in Britain, election to different representative bodies is through different electoral systems in which quotas are more or less easy to install. Elections to the presidency and the National Assembly are based on a majoritarian system that takes place in two stages. Parties compete for first and second positions in initial elections. Any party that receives more than 12.5 per cent of the potential vote is eligible to stand in the second round. In practice, however, negotiations take place within the right and the left in order to avoid split voting. In most constituencies the second round is a run-off election between the left and the right. However, sometimes the negotiations are unsuccessful, and then three parties may compete in the second round. Occasionally, negotiations lead to a one candidate 'election'. At local and departmental level, elections are fought in party list proportional systems. Women's advocates are organized who press for equality of women's political representation within French political parties. However, feminist activity outside the political parties appears to have been much more important. Although the main protagonists in the *parité* (parity) debates were party women, a considerable number of those debates took place in the wider public domain and especially in the media.

In France the movement for equality of women's representation really began in the 1970s, but did not gather much momentum until the 1990s. The obstacles included the familiar characteristics of institutional sexism, incumbent resistance and constitutional impediments (Allwood and Wadia 2000). Quotas were first constitutionalized in 1982 when the Conseil constitutionnel ruled against a law requiring that no more than 75 per cent of local electoral candidates should be of the same sex (Baudino 2005). Thereafter, French women's equality advocates were faced with the prospect of having to change the constitution.

According to Karen Bird, the decision of the constitutional court forced advocates of women's equality to develop a fundamental critique of French political arrangements and an appropriate strategy to change them. Their project was assisted by growing interest at the European and international levels in the political underrepresentation of women. French women claimed *parité*, which in effect is a 50 per cent quota. According to Baudino (2005), *parité* is a concept that is readily understood in French discourse, easily translatable and politically resonant. Quotas, on the other hand, are an English or American concept more difficult to translate. Advocates of *parité* made it clear that French women were underrepresented in politics not only in comparison to other countries but also by comparison to their position in other sectors of public life. By 1997, with only 6.1 per cent of the seats in the National Assembly and only 5.6 per cent in the Senate, French women had made no improvement in political representation since their enfranchisement in 1945.

The campaign was signalled by the publication of *Au Pouvoir Citoyennes! Liberté, egalité, parité* (Gaspard et al. 1992), soon followed by the publication of the *Manifeste des 577* in 1993 (577 is the number of seats in the National Assembly). Many organizations sprang up in support of *parité* in the ensuing years and by 1995 all three main presidential candidates included pledges for *parité* in their campaigns. After the 1995 presidential election had been won by RPR (Rally for the Republic) candidate Jacques Chirac, then Prime Minister Alain Juppé, also RPR, commissioned the *Observatoire de la parité* to report every two years on women's access to politics.

In June 1996, ten prominent French women politicians from different parties signed a public manifesto in support of *parité*. In 1996 the *Observatoire* recommended a constitutional revision to allow *parité* legislation to be passed. The Socialist Party acted after the change of government in 1998. Prime Minister Jospin was a supporter of *parité*. The government presented *parité* measures in the form of two constitutional amendments that were adopted in 1999 (Bird 2003). In June 2000 a law mandating the principal of equal access of women and men to political positions was passed.

In the meantime a widespread public debate that attracted daily media coverage saw prominent intellectuals making the cases for and against *parité*. Sylviane Agacinski (for) and Elisabeth Badinter (against) framed their debate as one about *la démocratie paritaire* v. *l'égalité universelle* in a classic French theoretical debate that saw the protagonists facing each other from opposite sides of newspaper pages. Both were married to men who were prominent in the Socialist Party and who were protagonists in the *parité* debate. The debates were most fierce within the parties, but were restricted to a small group of elite actors that included feminist advocates (Bird 2003).

As elsewhere, the devil is in the detail. The law established obligations and financial incentives for parties to nominate women candidates. Strong sanctions operated for elections that were held under PR – European, regional, municipal and some Senate constituencies. Parties were required to present gender-balanced lists with varying levels of strictness regarding the placement of women on the lists. Failure to comply meant that they could not register their list and so would be unable to contest the election. Moreover, for regional elections the law did not impose strict alternation between women and men candidates; rather, it required that women have three of every six places on lists (Baudino 2005; Bird 2003). For National Assembly elections, only financial incentives applied. A proportion of public funding was withheld from those parties that did not observe *parité*.

Where the law provided for strong sanctions, it worked. Party leaders had no difficulty in recruiting women candidates and it proved useful for leaders who wished to dislodge male incumbents. Women increased their shares of seats in municipal and departmental elections. The percentage of women holding local office in councils where the law applied rose from 22 to 48 per cent (Bird 2003; Murray 2003).

Even so, many municipal parties followed only the letter of the law, placing women in the bottom three of the first six positions on their lists. This placement meant that the election of women mayors, normally the person who comes first on the winning party's list, and also members of local cabinets, who are typically selected according to the order in which they are elected, was disappointing. Only 6.7 per cent of mayors elected in 2001 were women, a small rise from 4.4 per cent in the previous election (Bird 2003). Where the law was weak, women benefited very little. In National Assembly elections parties preferred to pay a financial penalty rather than ensure the election of women. Technically, parties

Examples: Quotas and Parité

Table 5.5 Post-*parité* electoral outcomes: National Assembly elections, 2002

Political party	Sex of winning candidate			
	Male	Female	Total	% Women
UMP	327	39	366	10.7
UDF	27	2	29	6.9
DVD	3	0	3	0
PS	124	24	148	16.2
PCF	18	4	22	18.2
Verts	2	1	3	33.3
DVG	4	1	5	20
Other	1	0	1	0
Total	506	71	577	12.3

Source: Murray 2003: 26

were able to resist the full implications of the law. Therefore only 12.3 per cent of deputies elected to the National Assembly in 2002 were women, a very small rise from the 10.2 per cent elected in 1997 (see table 5.5).

The complexities of post-*parité* elections are well described elsewhere (Baudino 2005; Bird 2003; Murray 2003). The consensus is that different implementing mechanisms and sanctions at various electoral levels go some way to explaining its different levels of success. The evidence suggests that throughout the system political parties did what they could to avoid nominating women for winnable seats (Bird 2003). However, some observers thought that in the case of the 2002 National Assembly elections, the disappointing results for women candidates were due to the unusual electoral circumstances. In 2002 the parties of the right won a landslide victory. The left, which nominated more women candidates, collapsed. The implication here is that had parties of the left done better, more women would have been elected. This expectation is supported by feminist research, which indicates that the victory of parties of the left leads to increases in the representation of women (Caul 1999). However this prediction does not work for France in 2002. Research by Rainbow Murray shows that, had the left won, only a small increase (from 12.3 per cent to 13.9 per cent) in the number of women deputies would have resulted. Murray replayed the 1997 election, placing women and men candidates in the seats they fought in 2002. It is clear from her work that all parties, including parties of the left, consistently placed women in unwinnable seats. Arguably then, in the 2002 National Assembly elections *parité* did not fail, because it was not implemented. Moreover, in contrast to Belgium, disappointing post-*parité* results have not led to an overhaul of regulations to ensure improvements in the future.

The French and UK examples have much in common. In both, political modernization and democratization arguments were opportunities used by feminists. In both, there was public support for refreshing the political class. In both, party political leaders took advantage of quotas to clear out their opponents. In both, international comparisons made the level of women's representation a public embarrassment. In both, right-wing politicians abstained from or were absent from decisions to change the law. In both, the mobilization of support was characterized by an expansion of feminist organization and capacity and location in strategic decision-making arenas.

However, there are important differences. The French notion of universal citizenship underpinned a discourse of entitlement that opened the way for increased women's representation without entitling other groups. The major players in the *parité* movement used justice arguments but ruled out important arguments about difference. They invoked traditions of republican civic unity. Their narrow outlook fits with French traditions of universal citizenship in which it was possible to argue that only women were eligible for group representation because women were the only category acknowledged to be excluded. Thus Bird (2003) argues that because *parité* law was not intended to deviate from republican traditions of civic unity, there was no expectation that women representatives would be different. In France, the *parité* decision was constitutionalized and in some elections it was compulsory. In Britain, the legislation was permissive and enabling, so few parties took advantage of it. In France, no major party implemented *parité*. In Britain, one major party implemented quotas.

Political Parties, Women's Mobilization and Quotas

France and Belgium excepted, in most European countries quota arrangements are made by party practice rather than electoral law. And in systems of party government, electoral law on candidate quotas is implemented through the parties. In western democracies quotas are devices that operate on and within political parties, where the strategy gains support for a variety of reasons. For example, quotas provide party leaders with the opportunity to clear out opponents and to refresh the political class with women activists whose politics are known and reliable. The quota and *parité* movements demonstrate the importance of political parties and the necessity for feminist mobilization. Feminist mobilization is not only part of the adoption process, it also affects implementation.

The capacity of women's movements to organize and influence candidate selection appears to have increased during the 1990s. This increase is evident in the British and French movements. The importance of organization within parties is well illustrated by both examples, although possibly in different ways. Internal party mobilization by feminists was strong in Britain at the implementation stage of reform but, whilst present, may not have been decisive in France. I am tentative about this statement because research on the French *parité* movement tends to focus on the debates that took place in public and the policy outcomes rather than on the roles of party women. Therefore, although tempting, it is not possible to generalize. However, the crucial lesson of the British Labour Party debates is that feminists cannot ignore political parties. Just as they are the main barriers to women, they are also the key institutions for increasing women's levels of representation.

The evidence that it is necessary for feminists to mobilize in political parties if they are to secure equality of political representation is overwhelming. In most Western European systems the experience of the 1980s and 1990s indicates that women make lasting political gains only when their voices are heard in party politics. In the wake of the new feminist movements of the 1970s, women demanded and secured party reforms with varying degrees of success. In some countries this led to the appearance of new issues in party programmes, new systems of candidate selection, new means of policy-making and the establishment of new structures of government such as ministries for women, equal opportunities ombudspersons and publicly funded women's committees. In response to pressure from women activists, members and voters, gender matters became explicit issues. These efforts had significant and lasting effects on party politics. Gradually, campaigns for equality gained support and parties began to respond. But the momentum built up by wide-ranging movements in support of equal rights would not have been enough to secure changes in party policies. Political parties moved on women's issues when they came under effective electoral pressure. In Greece, for example, particular parties took up women's issues when women's organizations became their affiliates (Cram 1994). In the USA the strong association of feminist movements with the Democratic Party is associated with a gender gap in voting whereby women more than men vote for the Democrats (Young 1996). Voting women have therefore become a constituency the Democratic Party cannot afford to offend.

Women's advocates have taken considerable advantage of opportunities to affect party politics. In general, once a party committed itself formally to the principle of gender equality in one sphere, then party women were able to use this commitment in their arguments for increased representation. Sweden is a good example of this sequence of claiming. Sweden has a widespread egalitarian ethos and several features of its electoral system favour women, but these cannot by themselves account for the increase that has occurred in women's representation at all levels of the system since the 1960s. There, it was women who changed, who made new claims on the party system. Within parties, four identifiable strategies were pursued. First, women's issues were brought to the political agenda. Prominent party women, supported by women's organizations and networks, raised issues of sex equality in the parties. Often they began with demands for policies to secure sex equality in employment, but the implications of equality for childcare, reproductive rights and family policies were also issues. Second, seeking to avoid accusations of sectionalism, they sought to transform women's issues into universal issues. Third, women used a dual strategy of working within women's networks and in male-dominated areas of the party. Finally, women paid close attention to the rules of the game. They sought to transform gender relations in politics from within, and were therefore careful to affirm their commitment to their parties (Sainsbury 1993).

The long march of women through party organizations has altered structures, rules and procedures. Thus parties have developed strategies to promote women internally into decision-making positions in the party organization and externally into elected assemblies and public appointments. Generally they have been more radical, determined and imaginative in devising policies to bring women into internal party positions than to nominate women as candidates for elected offices. The process tends to continue inexorably to candidate selection. Under pressure from women's advocates, research, awareness training and selection criteria changes bring more women into the recruitment pool, and thus strengthen demands to ensure their selection. Their most effective action has been the introduction of quotas of various kinds. Quotas are an effort to change the political equilibrium between women and men. Party quotas are normally voluntary both in the sense of not being guaranteed by legislation and because they are often not adequately backed by internal sanctions when targets are not met. Political parties are themselves voluntary organizations; there are therefore inevitable limitations on what can be done to implement controversial policies. Nevertheless, where political will has been present, usually when electoral stakes are apparent, political parties have been very effective in the implementation of quotas of women representatives.

The crucial arena for strategies to improve women's political representation in modern democracies is political parties. Such mobilization enhances the capacity of party women, thereby positioning them better to ensure that quotas are implemented. To exert influence, women's advocates must mobilize inside and outside parties to place maximum pressure on leaders to initiate and implement change. Quotas are not the only mechanism for achieving increases in the political presence of women. Rhetoric and promotion of equality have marked effects and are also part of the process of change. However, the decision to adopt and implement quotas is an important point in the process of establishing equal representation of women. It indicates a strong commitment to sex equality in politics.

6

Making a Difference?
Conclusions

The arguments so far have concentrated almost entirely on how to get equality of women's representation. When we ask the question 'What difference will women make to politics?', a further question immediately comes to mind: 'What kind of difference do we hope for?' In this concluding chapter I explore the question of what else happens when the number of women representatives changes, outlining the sources and implications of our explicit and implicit expectations of women politicians. First, I describe the expectations that have been raised by feminist theory. Second, I assess prospects for change in the light of the predictions suggested by the feminist study of political institutions and argue that a feminist institutionalism could offer realistic analysis of presence effects. I then examine both the movements for presence in Britain and the press response to it, for promises that women will make a difference. Having established the sources of our expectations of women representatives, on the basis of British experience, I assess the evidence that women politicians have made a difference.

Theories and Effects

Two overlapping ideas dominate the discussion of the effects of increasing women's political representation – the notion of critical mass and the politics of 'presence'. 'Presence' provides the basis of a theory of gender difference and political representation while the notion of critical mass has been used as a descriptive indicator of the proportion of women required to make a substantial difference to politics. Iris Marion Young and Anne Phillips have advanced theories of the politics of presence in arguments situated in critiques of theories of democratic politics. Both explicitly and implicitly, the theories include consideration of how and why an equalization of the numbers of men and women representatives make it likely that other changes will take place. Making the case for positive action to equalize the representation of women and men, Anne Phillips argues that women's experiences could not be addressed in a politics dominated by men. Acknowledging that mechanisms of accountability (the politics of ideas) will still be required in a representative democracy, she argues nevertheless that the distinctive needs and interests of women require representation by women (Phillips 1995, 1999). Her argument implies that women have shared common interests that will be considered in political decision-making only if women are present. The argument asserts gender difference and details its relevance to politics, claiming that women's interests exist and that such interests merit representation. Although she claims that the presence of women will almost certainly affect the deliberation of representatives, Phillips does not engage the empirical question of how many women are necessary for 'presence' to be meaningful.

Presence theory is widely cited but little empirically tested. How many women are necessary to ensure their interests are considered? There is an overlap of the idea of critical mass and the idea of presence. However, there are crucial differences – notably that presence theory considers how and why changes might follow from equality of representation. By contrast, the idea of critical mass is a metaphor derived from nuclear physics and much used in the US sociology of race relations in the 1960s and 1970s. It signifies the amount of nuclear material that is needed to begin a chain reaction and is invoked to describe rather than theorize the effects of changing numbers of women in politics. Feminist advocates invoked it in the 1980s as a shorthand term to explain why the few women then in legislatures behaved so similarly to male legislators. Gradually the term became more widely used in discussions of how many women were needed to make a difference. Famously, Rosabeth Moss Kanter (1977) examined the effect of numbers on gender relations in an industrial corporation. She identified four categories of numbers. *Uniform* groups contain only men or women. *Skewed* groups contain a large imbalance of men or women, up to about 15 per cent of the minority group. *Tilted* groups contain about 15–40 per cent of the opposite sex. Lastly, *balanced* groups contain 40–50 per cent of each sex. Kanter was explicitly interested in numbers. Her emphasis was on the changing position of the token as its size in relation to the dominant group changed. She did not use the term 'critical mass', but her ideas were similar. She suggested the term 'tipping point' to indicate the number at which the position of the token tips the balance between token and dominant groups.

As with Kanter's 'tipping points', the idea of critical mass is that the nature of group interactions depends on their relative size. When a group remains a distinct minority within a larger society, its members are tokens who will seek to adapt to their surroundings, conforming to the predominant rules of the game. They will not act to increase the size of their group. If anything, their various available strategies (queen bee, assimilation, etc.) will tend to keep the number of tokens appropriately small. But once the group reaches a certain size, available strategies change. The change is qualitative, altering the nature of group interactions, as the minority starts to assert itself and thereby transform the institutional culture, norms and values.

In Kanter's theory, numbers are central and affect relationships between tokens and dominants in the same way regardless of whether the difference between tokens and dominants is race, class, gender or some other social category. Her work is very much of its time and was later criticized by Janice Yoder in a landmark article in the journal *Gender and Society* (1991). Yoder argues that gender is a unique social category. She reasons that the effects described by Kanter occur only when women join gender inappropriate occupations (according to traditional divisions of labour). She also points out that Kanter's theory fails to anticipate backlash, which other research shows is especially likely in response to 'surges' of women. 'Backlash' may impede the progress of the rising group in an organization. Because Kanter missed important patterns of response to increases in the numbers of women, she could not explain why changes in women's presence impact on the gender regime of an institution.

Yoder argued that Kanter's work and the research it inspired attributes consequences to numbers when they should be attributed to a process – in this case, sexism. A concentration on numbers conflates workplace gender ratios, gender status, norms of occupational appropriateness, patterns of resistance and intrusiveness. These are separate elements of an institution's gender regime, each of which may have different and conflicting effects. To assess the *impact* of changes in numbers, it is necessary to have an appreciation of the *context* in which numbers are changing. This includes procedure, modes of communication, institutional mores and informal processes. In general, an understanding of the institution is necessary if we are to assess properly the impact of changing the numbers of women who are part of it.

The use of critical mass in arguments about women's representation is an oversimplification that raises expectations about its effects. The term suggests there is an identifiable point at which a recognizable difference occurs. However, the kind of difference that women's representation could make and the reasons for such differences are not part of its theorization. The term is frequently used in popular discussions of politics, most often to explain why women politicians have not made the difference that they will surely make as soon as there are enough of them. Despite the difficulties entailed by its use and its apparent closing out of modern theories of gender relations, the idea of critical mass continues to have some popular purchase and has also attracted other research. It has come to be one of those quasi-scientific terms used to give weight to what are essentially rhetorical points.

In the first systematic attempt to operationalize the concept of critical mass in a study of women's political representation, Drude Dahlerup rejected it in favour of her theory of 'minority representation'. This explained the behaviour and effects of Nordic women legislators in the 1980s. Based on interviews with politicians, Dahlerup's research identified a number of areas in which women legislators could make a difference and she itemized the differences they thought they had made (1988).

Dahlerup's research predates the development of presence theory, which includes a consideration of how change occurs. It suggests that, as the numbers of women change, so also will other elements of the legislature because men and women bring different values, priorities and styles to politics and those differences have political consequences of various kinds. These consequences are not specified. However, there is some agreement about what they *might* be. Increasing the presence of women is variously expected to change the institutional culture, the agenda (output), the styles and the procedures of the legislature. Most accounts forecast gradual change, few accounts describe the processes of change.

Such processes are likely to be institution-specific and will vary by political system. The effects are path-dependent. By this I mean that a great deal depends on what has gone before. The potential of women's representation is likely to be greatly affected by such institutional considerations, but they are rarely taken into account. For example, in most

Western European systems, party government means that activity to increase women's representation and the effects of its increase are first and foremost felt within parties. Changes in each political party are shaped by its rules, ideology and culture. Party women will then enter the legislature. They will be carriers of gender change that has already been shaped by parties. In time, and in a similar way, changes in the legislature take place that are shaped by its pre-existing institutional culture, rules and practices. Thus there are at least three elements to an understanding of the effects of increasing the numbers of women representatives. First, we must look for change in the right places – in a legislature, a party group within a legislature, and in the party proper. In Western European systems of party government, the first object of institutional study must be the party group. Social and cultural changes in gender relations will probably appear in political parties before they are manifest in the legislature. The second requirement is that we characterize the culture of the relevant institution in terms of gender. The third requirement is that we appreciate how the institutions shape the behaviour of women representatives. Here we must be alert to how gender itself is created and recreated in the various institutions.

In the absence of institutionally sensitive theories of gender-politics, and gender-sensitive theories of political institutions, it is almost impossible to answer questions that arise from concerns about whether women make a difference. We might, of course, contest the question itself, and argue that it is unjustified (the justice strategy). But the temptation to try to respond will remain. Answering the question about the difference women representatives make requires that presence theory is integrated with theories of institutional change. Modern institutional approaches to the study of politics can be combined with gender theory using the concepts of gender regimes described in chapter 2.

To explain further, it is necessary to consider again the nature of political institutions and how gender relations may affect them. Institutions are the 'formal rules, compliance procedures and standard operating practices that structure relationships between individuals in various units of the polity and the economy' (Hall 1986: 19–20). Political institutions 'express particular choices about how political relationships ought to be shaped; they are in the nature of continuing injunctions to members of society that they should try to conduct themselves in specific ways when engaged in the pursuit of political ends. This is to define political institutions as necessarily containing a normative element' (Oakeshott, quoted in Rhodes 1995: 47). The normative order is the prevailing 'ideological proscriptions and prescriptions' – that is, the norms, principles and ideas – that hold a given institutional structure together and provide the 'compass' for the assessments of attempts at change. This order consists of collectively constructed values and principles that must be protected and put into effect. These norms are exemplified by the formal and informal rules of the game and the fundamental mechanisms whereby the rules are made and implemented. These rules (a) take precise meaning through the actions of the individual organizations (parliaments, executives and political parties) that they constitute and (b) structure, largely but imperfectly, the interactions that take place between and within these organizations (March and Olsen 1989: 107).

The most consistent prediction of institutional theory is that institutions are able to resist change. This means that established gender norms are protected. Historically, legislatures have been white, male, middle- and upper-class spaces in which political decisions were taken. Within those spaces norms of behaviour were established, often over centuries of repetition. Those norms are saturated with gender, racial and class assumptions.

One of the normative elements embedded in the House of Commons is a culture of masculinity that is based on white middle-class male assumptions about what it is to be a representative, an MP. It is built on often unspoken assumptions about a traditional gendered division of labour and was shaped over centuries in which no women were present. The practices and procedures that developed constitute a particular gender regime that is hostile to women and femininity and supportive only of traditional forms of femininity in which women are not present as legislators, but as cleaners, caterers and, of course, wives of legislators. The regime is manifested in rules, procedures, discourses and practices with which many men are comfortable and most women are not. Requirements for masculine dress (top hats, neckties), provision for hanging up one's sword but none for looking after one's child, admiration for demagoguery and conflict, adversarial styles of debate, a chamber whose acoustics favour loud voices, the frequent use of military metaphors, the regularly reported experience of women MPs barred by staff from 'Member only' areas are all manifestations of the gender regime of the UK Parliament. In addition, overt sexist behaviour was characteristic of male MPs in the debating chamber and throughout the Palace of Westminster.

When newly elected 'others' arrive at Westminster they disrupt the established norms – in this case, of white masculinity. Nirmal Puwar (2004) writes that the very presence of others – that is, non-male and non-white representatives – is disruptive because it draws attention to the hidden expectations that an MP is a particular kind of man. Puwar untangles, identifies and describes some of the processes that attend the entry of others, whom she terms 'space invaders', into white male institutional territory. Disorientation occurs because the invader is not the norm, because there is an 'element of surprise in seeing people who belong elsewhere'. For example, in the late 1990s, when Puwar conducted her research, new 'black' and women MPs were quite commonly told that they should not be in a 'Members only' bar or lift. Disorientation is compounded by 'amplification of numbers', through which a small number of women may be imagined as a large, overwhelming group, thus exaggerating their possible impact. Infantalization also occurs. Infantalization is the attribution of lower levels of competence and status to the incomer. The invaders bear a 'burden of doubt' that they may not be good enough and a 'burden of representation' that any of their mistakes will be attributed to their entire group. Thus women representatives are highly aware that judgements of their performance are judgements of the capacity of all women to be MPs. Super-surveillance, whereby the behaviour of the invaders is closely observed and (often harshly) judged, takes place (Puwar 2004).

Westminster is a particularly tough case. However, the processes that Puwar describes are typical of the processes that inhibit the ability of women representatives to change political institutions. By the time women arrive in established legislatures, particular norms of masculinity have become a template according to which incomers are socialized. As Puwar writes:

> The position of an MP has been performed as a highly masculinist act. Relations are organised on the basis of patronage, hierarchical fraternising and competitive individual exhibitionism. Gangs, blocks and allegiances are formed to offer support in a system of patronage and combat. Displays of masculinity in the House of Commons are conducted in a spectacular, exaggerated and theatrical manner . . . the hero of this performance is a white male . . . this is the template against which the speech, gestures and bodily movements of female and black and Asian bodies are measured. (2004: 74–5)

The pressure to conform to the template is almost overwhelming, but its styles and forms are not readily adopted by those who are not white, male and middle class. The script is appropriate for those who wrote it, but grotesque when read by others. Gender and racial expectations intervene and interfere. Thus women MPs are subject to conflicting pressures. They are expected to conform to institutional norms and to display acceptable feminine characteristics (Puwar 2004). However, they must not be too feminine. Women are required to perform a balancing of masculinity and femininity that is so finely tuned that it is a wonder that elected women continue to show up in the House of Commons, let alone stand for re-election.

Puwar's account both highlights the nature of the Westminster gender regime and alerts us to the requirements of feminist analysis of political institutions. Her work vividly illustrates the effects that women might have in a political institution. It confirms that it is necessary to take account of the procedures and culture in which decision-making takes place and of the everyday activities and behaviour through which the gender regime is expressed.

Broadly speaking, the theoretical arguments about the impact of women representatives suggest that any optimism about the changes their entry might bring should be tempered. However, raising expectations of change is part of the process by which increases in women's political representation is achieved. Even when we know what to expect, we may well have already come to expect too much.

Voting and Expectations of Women

The campaigns for quotas and parity discussed in chapters 4 and 5 were mobilizations of women who were no longer prepared to accept traditional gendered divisions of political labour. However, claims were located in political practices that affected the way they developed. Long-term changes in women's voting behaviour enabled campaigners to argue that gender gaps showed that women's votes were a prize that parties could no longer take for granted. In many countries, long-standing gender gaps, whereby women were more likely than men to vote for parties of the right, were a political given. During the 1980s this pattern began to change. In the United States women shifted their support from the Republican to the Democratic Party, while men moved towards the Republican Party. Gender dealignment also occurred in many

Western European countries. These patterns have been extensively researched and found by Inglehart and Norris to be worldwide phenomena (2003).

Gender realignment may have the capacity to change the rules of the political game. To court women voters, political parties try to feminize their image, their manifestos and their personnel. In this process, what is most interesting about the gender gap in voting is not so much its existence, with which most people are now familiar, but how it has been used by feminist advocates to claim representation. From the late 1980s, women's advocates in the UK used gender gap evidence as a platform from which to argue for presence. The voting patterns were fairly straightforward. A gender gap in voting was a feature of UK electoral behaviour from 1945 to 1992. Comparing women's and men's responses to surveys of voting, Pippa Norris confirmed a long-standing gender gap in which women were more likely to vote Conservative. The Conservative advantage peaked in the 1950s, fluctuated during the 1960s and 1970s and closed to insignificance in the 1980s, only to reopen in 1992 when the gap was greatest among older women while younger women actually preferred Labour (Norris 1999). A gender generation gap, in which younger women moved towards Labour while older women continued to be Conservative, persisted through the 1990s. Prominent Labour women drew attention to the party's deficit among women voters from the 1980s onward. The party's traditional masculine image, its culture, its style, its language and its male dominance were all cited as being off-putting to women voters. In the run-up to the 1997 election, activity was especially intense. A group called Winning Words met regularly to consider how to feminize Labour's electoral appeal. Deborah Mattinson and Patricia Hewitt presented the findings of the group to the shadow cabinet in 1996 (Lovenduski 1998). The party women's office and the NEC women's committee funded focus groups that discovered the causes of Labour's failure to appeal to women. Language, style and image were all found to be implicated. Equality advocates were successful at convincing the party of the need to attract women's votes by altering language, appearance and style and, for example, by using outlets such as daytime television and women's magazines to put policies across.

In the course of this process it was repeatedly argued that feminizing the parliamentary party would appeal to women voters. The argument was straightforward. More women candidates and MPs would bring the kind of image and style that were needed to get more votes. The expectation was met. In 1997 the swing to Labour was larger among women than among men (Kellner 1997). However, once in power, Labour forgot the gender lessons of the 1997 victory.

Women's advocates continued their argument. Between 1997 and 2001 the gender gap was regularly invoked as a way of placing pressure on the party. Opinion polls showed that women were less satisfied with the government than men. A widely reported study by Deborah Mattinson revealed that 16 per cent more women than men were dissatisfied with the government, a figure that could translate into a million votes. Mattinson reported her findings to a high-level policy seminar attended by senior party figures in 2000. She told them that 'women are less loyal to any party than men, less tribal and more likely to be floating voters. Knowing all this we have to assume the women's vote is vulnerable' (*The Sunday Times*, 16 April 2000, p. 15; Harman and Mattinson 2000). Press reports gave the gender gap considerable attention throughout 2000 and early 2001 (see, for example, Michael Prescott, 'The nannying tendency, *The Sunday Times*, 16 April 2000; Martin Walker, 'Men, again', *Guardian*, 27 June 2000; Polly Toynbee, 'Time for a sex change', *Guardian*, 29 September 2000; Rosemary Bennett, 'Women voters may snub Hague', *Financial Times*, 2 May 2001).

The gender gap was also used to place pressure on the other political parties where similar arguments took place. Women's advocates in the Conservative Party drew attention to the party's lack of appeal to women voters. A report by Tessa Keswick (Director of the Centre for Policy Studies and

former special adviser to Ken Clarke and a Conservative parliamentary candidate), Rosemary Pockley (former vice-chair
of the Conservative Women's National Committee) and
Angela Guillaume (former chair of the European Union of
Women) drew attention to the defection of women voters
from the Conservative Party. Both justice and pragmatic
arguments were invoked. They called for urgent and radical
change on grounds of both fairness and expediency and
argued for the implementation of effective strategies to field
more women candidates in winnable seats. A report by Fiona
Buxton of the Bow group made a similar case (Buxton 2000).
The arguments were revisited in all the parties after the 2001
general election, when turnout, including that of women, fell
dramatically.

The appeal of political parties to women voters has become
a mainstay of UK political journalism, a recurring, standard-
ized story in which women's dissatisfaction with politics and
the government is noted, often from surveys devised especially for that purpose. The implied solution is more women
politicians. Candidate selection is tracked in the major parties by journalists who make connections between women
politicians and electoral appeal to women in discussions of
the difficulties parties have in selecting more women as
candidates for winnable seats. The failure of the Labour and
Conservative parties to select women is a recurring story most
often considered in terms of its possible effects on women's
votes (Lucy Ward, 'Labour's women MPs aim for the female
voter', *Guardian*, 23 June 2000; Gabby Hinscliff, 'Blair loses
appeal to women', *Observer*, 4 February 2000; Nicholas
Watt, 'Labour slipping in the equality race', *Guardian*,
16 October 2000). The Conservatives receive the same treatment (Lucy Ward, 'It's the party of the family – shouldn't
you be at home looking after the children?' *Guardian*,
25 March 1999; Rosemary Bennet, 'Women voters may snub
Hague', *Financial Times*, 5 February 2001; Julia Hartley
Brewer, ' "Old fashioned" Tories urged to woo back women',
Guardian, 12 November 1999).

This journalism did not happen by accident. During the 1990s women's advocates became adept at political communications. Fawcett, in particular, developed an effective press strategy in which sympathetic journalists were cultivated. Research framed in terms of standard political narratives was commissioned, then offered as exclusives to key journalists and launched at well-publicized press conferences and by means of sophisticated press releases and statements by the society's director. Fawcett repeatedly used gender gap data to make its case for women's political representation. In short, women's advocates used the gender gap to place pressure on parties to feminize politics. They made links between substantive and descriptive representation of women; they used pragmatic arguments to suggest that fair representation of women would bring an electoral reward. These interventions were, and are, clever politics.

Internal party debates about quotas of candidates are similarly framed. Moreover, after 1997 the presence of women became a necessary part of the modern image that parties wanted to present. For example, women's representation became associated with democracy in the new Scottish Parliament. However by making outright claims that women will make a difference, or even making simple juxtapositions of presence and difference, the expectations of elected women politicians are raised. This therefore becomes part of the process of winning support for women's representation. Such expectations may take little account of what is actually possible in the legislature.

Backlash: A Form of Institutional Resistance

Incomers can expect to meet resistance not only in the legislature but also in the form of widespread and popular backlash to their presence and performance. This was the experience of the new Labour women MPs newly elected in 1997. The backlash after that election was of considerable duration and full of venom. It is illustrative of how, on the one hand, women politicians are expected to make a difference and are criticized for not transforming centuries of male-designed traditions of politics. But, on the other hand, they are expected to fit in with the culture of the institution and prove themselves according to criteria developed during its long history as a male institution.

After 1997 the new women MPs came under enormous scrutiny. A very damaging photograph of the 101 Labour women surrounding Tony Blair in front of Parliament was captioned 'Blair's Babes'. The term stuck. It seemed as though an open war was declared on these women. The New Labour government operated a very strict party discipline according to which only dependable speakers were called on to speak in debates. Whilst experienced MPs could get the Speaker's attention, new members were especially reliant on arrangements made for them by their party whips. To increase one's chance of speaking and to gain the approval of party leaders, backbench MPs agreed to ask 'planted questions' that would provide the opportunity for the government to report its successes. Both women and men participated in the practice, but the women were singled out for particular criticism. The male-dominated press colluded. The unfortunate Helen Brinton became the subject of particular attack by *Guardian* columnist Matthew Norman, who continues his offensive against her to this day (see, e.g. *Guardian*, 10 September 2003). Others were regularly mocked by the parliamentary correspondents, who earned their living by making jokes about political events.

The correspondents are very influential. Jackie Ashley has described a process in which (male) parliamentary correspondents meet for long and liquid lunches during which they decide what the joke of the day will be. In a familiar process of egging each other on, the correspondents develop and refine the joke, usually at the expense of an individual politician. The joke will then form part of the next day's columns (Ashley 2002). The newspaper-reading majority is not aware of the source of the joke but understands that the person whose victim it is appears at best ridiculous and at worst selfish, stupid and ambitious.

The shared nature of the joke is visible only to those who read all the papers and take note of what is in all of the columns (mainly other journalists). Journalists throughout the media get a good deal of their information from other journalists. One effect is that other stories are framed by the insights of the columnists. After the lone mothers benefit vote took place, special venom was reserved by journalists for 'Blair's Babes', who were, amongst other things, accused of being stupid (Libby Purves, 'Blair's Babes in the Wood', *The Times*, 2 December 1997; Leader, *Independent on Sunday*, 4 January 1998) and careerist (*Guardian*, 29 April 1998).

The sexism of the correspondents reflected and refracted sexism in the chamber. Labour MP Brian Sedgemore referred to the new women MPs as the 'Stepford Wives' (6 February 1998) and Ann Widdecombe said the comment was insulting to Stepford Wives. Both comments were widely reported and have frequently been cited since. The syndrome of vilification continued throughout the first Labour government. Thus Catherine Bennett of the *Guardian* (3 August 2000) attacked 'Millbankettes' for their engagement with parliamentary modernization, stating that their only interest was in reforming their own working conditions. Bennett is a lifestyle columnist paid to amuse readers with sarcasm rather than to offer political insight. Her use of the story is an indication of how embedded the view of the new women became. Other stories trivialized women's concerns.

Examples of the harsh treatment of the new women MPs abound. Within Parliament, resistance reflected the sexism of the culture. An early effort to allow and provide breast-feeding facilities for nursing mothers in the House of Commons met with obdurate opposition from the Speaker, Betty Boothroyd. Women MPs complained of their treatment by male colleagues. Some were propositioned by drunken colleagues and confronted with the language and gestures of explicit sexism. According to Julia Drown, 'most people recognise that women get more barracking. The noise level definitely goes up when a woman gets up to speak' (*Independent*, 6 August 2001). When she announced her plans to resign after only one term Tess Kingham wrote about how she had looked forward to her job as an MP. She thought her work would bring her to the centre of political debate and involve detailed scrutiny of legislation. Instead, she found 'mock combat' between government and opposition. The combat was embodied by opposition MPs 'endlessly thrusting their groins around'. Moreover, resistance came not only from opposition men but also from women who undermined the incoming women MPs. For example, their calls for reform and modernization of parliamentary working hours were misrepresented to suggest that the women modernizers were unprofessional and not up to the job (Kingham 2001).

Inevitably the atmosphere described by Kingham inhibited the new women MPs. The daily reassertion and repetitions of inappropriate, dated and sexist values were, and are, a strategy of resistance to change.

What do we know about the effects of women's presence in legislatures? So far, I have argued that legislatures are gender regimes that women are expected to change against considerable resistance. Nevertheless changes did take place in attitudes, behaviour and policies. These changes need to be considered in context. To illustrate the effects that women might have within a particular gender regime, it is necessary to take account of the procedures and culture in which decision-making takes place. The process can be conceptualized as a series of steps. Presence theory implies that the necessary first step in determining whether an increase in the number of women representatives will make a difference to politics is to establish that gender differences exist and to suggest a shared women's interest. The second is to demonstrate that such differences are to be found among politicians. Institutional theory suggests that the third is to examine how processes are shaped by the gendered culture of the legislature.

The first step, though obviously necessary, is difficult. I described in chapter 2 some of the difficulties of identifying women's interests. In her writing about Swedish legislators, Lena Wängnerud has explained how the concept of women's interest is both common and controversial in feminist scholarship. Problems include the relationship between objective and subjective interests and the relationships between gender and other social divisions (Wängnerud 2000: 68). Wängnerud argues that using a strong definition of women's interests best treats such problems. Accordingly, following a well-worn path in feminist debates about the welfare state, she declares women's shared interest to be in increasing their autonomy, a process that requires *'the politicisation of women's every day life experiences to the same extent as those of men'* (2000: 70; my emphasis). Implicitly, such politicization brings new issues to the political agenda, alters priorities and leads to the politicization or (greater politicization) of issues that mainly affect women, such as sex equality policy, reproductive rights and childcare.

Women's interests are served by a process in which the gender regimes of a political institution alter. Simply, women's issues are ones that are more likely to affect women than men. Gendered issues are those that differentially affect men and women. Part of the process of the politicization of women's everyday life experiences is precisely the political recognition, discussion and mediation of such differences. Such politicization is another process that can be treated as a number of steps in which, first, women are recognized as a social category, that is, the gender neutrality of normal politics is contested. Second, the inequalities of power between the sexes are acknowledged and, third, policies to increase the autonomy of women are made. In her analysis of interview data on successive cohorts of Swedish legislators, Wängnerud shows how each step influenced various stages of the political process. She concludes that women's presence in the Riksdag brought about a shift of emphasis in politics whereby women's interests became more central. She found differences in attitudes between women and men across a range of issues and showed how these differences provoked political changes that led to an increased legislative sensitivity to women's interests by all politicians. The articulation and mobilization of those interests in the Riksdag was the work of women politicians (Wängnerud 2000).

Attitude Change

In Wängnerud's approach, tests of presence effects are therefore tests of the changes in values, attitudes, styles and substance that accompany increases or decreases in the presence of women in a legislature. Styles are notoriously difficult to quantify (however, we might use interview items on men's and women's notions of what the job involves and their attitudes to parliamentary reform as a measure). Values and priorities can be tested using standard survey techniques. It is clearly not enough to show that the values and priorities of women entrants differ from those of men when we consider if change in the gender regime has resulted from an increase in the numbers of women legislators. It is also necessary to show that differences exist. Strictly, it is also necessary to show that such differences become more pronounced as the number of women representatives increases. Such differences are a necessary but not sufficient condition of the presence effect in politics.

Are such differences in men's and women's values present in the British House of Commons? Testing the effects of feminization in Parliament has only recently become possible. Research on parliamentary candidates and MPs in the 1992 and 1997 elections found that when compared with men within each party, women were slightly more supportive of feminist and left-wing values, expressed stronger concern about social policy issues, and gave higher priority to constituency casework. However, the numbers were small and in all cases the gender gap was modest. Overall it was political party rather than gender that proved the strongest predictor of values and attitudes (Norris and Lovenduski 1995; Norris 1996; Norris 2000).

Did the situation change after the entry of a new cohort of women politicians? In 1997 women shifted from being a 'skewed' to a 'tilted' group in the House of Commons. At 24 per cent of the Parliamentary Labour Party, women were a substantial minority, in a position to have an effect. In Kanter's terms, the change was from a token number towards a minority strong enough to affect the nature of the wider group. This, as I argued above, is not a simple effect of 'numbers' but involves processes. Members of tilted groups are able to form alliances and act as a coherent force. These processes may position them to affect the dominant culture of their institution and to perform the 'critical' acts that Dahlerup (1988) argues are necessary to the feminization of political institutions. Processes of 'making a difference' have a logical progression. If women MPs are to represent women's interests, they must recognize and support such interests and then act accordingly. Attitudes are logically prior to action, hence analysis of effects must start with an analysis of attitudes.

British studies consistently indicate that women and men differ in their attitudes towards sex equality. These attitude differences are found among legislators. British Representation Study data confirm that whilst politicians' attitudes are similar on some issues, they differ by sex in their attitudes to positive action and liberal sex equality policy. The differences appear across the political spectrum. When MPs' attitudes towards sex equality across a range of issues are compared, there are sex differences in each party and also differences between political parties. Labour Party and Liberal Democratic Party women MPs are more supportive of equality than men, Labour Party women are more in favour of sex equality measures than Liberal Democrats, Liberal Democrat women are more supportive than are Conservative Party women.

There may also be evidence that support for sex equality increased as the number of women grew. After 1992, among all MPs and within each party group, successive surveys of MPs' attitudes demonstrated the existence of sex differences in attitudes to women's interests. In addition they showed that support for sex equality grew as the number of women legislators increased. This evidence indicates that women MPs in all the major British parties have a different set of values from men on issues affecting women's equality, in the workplace, home and public sphere. Whilst these attitude differences are not dramatic, they are consistent and they suggest change. Potentially these attitudes may be translated into party manifestos, political debate and, ultimately, legislative action. They may shape policies towards equal pay, reproductive rights and the adoption of affirmative action strategies in the recruitment of women within parties. If their attitudes to sex equality are translated into action, then the entry of more women leaders into Westminster has the capacity to make a difference to public policy (Lovenduski and Norris 2003).

In summary, attitude research shows that the preconditions for making a difference to British politics are present. The attitudes of women MPs are associated with identifiable components of women's interests. The British evidence shows that women representatives are more divided by party on most issues than they are by sex, but are more supportive of equal opportunities than men, a finding that has been repeated in other countries and at other levels of the British political system (Mateo-Diaz 2002; Wängnerud 2000).

Institutional Change

There were many new faces after the 1997 general election, and the turnover of MPs was very high. There were 259 (out of 659) new MPs, 65 of whom were women. Labour women MPs networked and met in the Labour Party Parliamentary

Women's Group. The new women learned the rules of the House and the realities of party discipline, working within a huge majority party as the new government bedded in.

The most immediate and visible change after 1997 was in the composition of government. Growth in the number of women representatives permitted growth in the number of women in cabinet posts. Previous cabinets had included one or, at the most, two women. After 1997 five women were appointed to Tony Blair's first cabinet, and a women's minister was appointed (very belatedly and only after a reminder from women MPs and party officials). In terms of personnel, however, the feminization of government was notable. Between 1997 and 2001, 35 women served on the front benches – 26 MPs in the Commons and 9 in the House of Lords. Although no Labour woman has so far held any of the four top positions in government (Prime Minister, Chancellor of the Exchequer, Foreign Secretary, Home Secretary), since 1997 many women ministers have served in government positions that were previously thought of as male. These appointments depended upon a pool of able women in the House of Commons.

The structure of government also altered as government agencies charged with acting for women were created and 'upgraded'. Government has included women's equality machinery since 1969, when the Women's National Commission (WNC), with responsibility for ensuring consultation between government and women's organizations, was first established. The Equal Opportunities Commission (EOC) was set up as a cross-sectional agency with responsibility to oversee the sex equality legislation by the Sex Discrimination Act of 1975. From 1986 a ministerial group on women's issues operated under the aegis of the Home Office. In 1992 it became a cabinet committee, its brief to consider women's issues on a cross-sectional basis. A succession of cabinet members were given the 'women's portfolio' in addition to their other responsibilities, which they sometimes accepted only reluctantly (Lovenduski and Randall 1993).

The new Ministry for Women took over responsibility for much of the sex equality machinery and the minister worked with a cabinet committee on women, later termed the Women and Equality Committee, to signify concern with other equalities, such as homosexual rights. The women's portfolio has been held by a cabinet member since 1997. However, it has yet to be her primary responsibility. Since the creation of the Ministry there have normally been two 'ministers for women', one at cabinet level and a junior minister who takes day-to-day responsibility for women's equality issues.

Government ambivalence towards the Ministry has been apparent from the outset. The first cabinet-level minister for women, Harriet Harman, was also Secretary of State for Social Security. Her appointment was widely understood to be an afterthought, as her 'women's responsibilities' were announced some time after her initial appointment (Lovenduski 1997). Her work was supported by Joan Ruddock, MP, who acted as her unpaid PPS.[1] When Harman was sacked (taking Ruddock with her), Baroness Margaret Jay, who was also leader of the House of Lords, succeeded her and Tessa Jowell took over the role of spokesperson for women in the Commons. The reception to these appointments was mixed. Whilst Jowell had a record of equality advocacy, Margaret Jay was openly disdainful of feminism. After the 2001 elections, Patricia Hewitt was appointed minister for women and Secretary of State for Trade and Industry and the junior position was held initially by Sally Morgan, Blair's influential political adviser. In order to be eligible to be minister, Morgan had first to be appointed to the House of Lords (she was not an MP). However, she resigned her post after a few months to become the Prime Minister's personal assistant, and was replaced by Barbara Roche until 2003, when Jacqui Lait was

1 Ruddock was unpaid because by the time she was appointed, the budget for government salaries had been allocated. Her unpaid status was taken as one of many indications that the Blair government was not serious about the portfolio.

appointed. Sally Morgan is widely believed by women MPs to be an effective advocate of women's rights in Downing Street. The appointment of women's ministers has sent mixed messages about government preferences. Harman, Hewitt, Lait, Morgan and Ruddock are feminists who had been active in the party movement to increase women's representation. Roche and Jay are not feminists; both went to some trouble to distance themselves from the term.

In Labour's first term the Ministry for Women had a poor reputation. Government did not value it, and it was also remote from many of the feminist activists who had campaigned for its installation, and poor at communications. The unit was threatened at the end of the first Labour government when there were rumours of plans to abolish it. An intensive campaign by feminists called for its retention. After 2001, its status, budget, effectiveness and communications improved. However, the Women's Unit was renamed the Women and Equality Unit in 2001, one of many signals that it was to be amalgamated with other agencies. In 2002 the government minister for women, Barbara Roche, announced that Westminster equality bodies were to be reviewed with the aim of creating a single cross-sectional grouping that would bring together responsibility for the various equality agencies and the new requirements of the Amsterdam Treaty. Plans to establish a new Commission for Equality and Human Rights were confirmed in May 2004 with the publication of the White Paper, *Fairness for All*. The organizational logic of this amalgamation is obvious if we think that one equality is pretty much like another. However, one equality does not appear to be pretty much like another in terms of government priorities. The initiative has been sharply criticized by women's advocates, who fear that gender issues will fare badly in competition for priority within the combined agency (Squires and Wickham-Jones 2004).

Between 1997 and 2004, the unit was located in the Department of Social Security, the Cabinet Office, the Office of the Deputy Prime Minister and the Department of Trade and

Industry (DTI). It has followed its ministers and has been unable to secure a reliable place in a government department. It does not have credibility with senior civil servants and does not have the capacity to do its job of gender mainstreaming which requires, amongst other things, that it must influence hostile government officials. On any assessment, its position is unpromising. Because it is a weak institution, the Women's 'Ministry' does not provide convincing evidence of institutional change. Indeed, its fortunes may indicate that it exists largely for cosmetic reasons. At the outset the unit was given insufficient power and authority. Its remit was unclear and it was a low priority for government. The continuing problems, as outlined by Judith Squires and Mark Wickham-Jones (2004), are threefold. First, institutional uncertainty has been a continuing feature of the status of the unit. Second, its remit has been broad, which has made it difficult to find a focus and identity. Third, the unit is required to secure the cooperation of non-feminists in the decision-making process. It does not have implementation capacity.

To some extent, the problems of the Women and Equality Unit were to be expected. Institutional theory predicts that it will be some years before an authoritative assessment of the impact of the 1997 'breakthrough' by women is possible. Feminist research similarly indicates that some time must elapse before significant institutional change is apparent. Feminist institutional theory predicts considerable resistance to changes in gender regimes. This is borne out in Parliament. The mere presence of new women did not displace the template of masculinity. The realities were instructive. The cohort of new women MPs soon learned that their room for manoeuvre was limited. Many new entrants were elected unexpectedly and their position was insecure, with many in marginal seats. Party discipline, the inexperience of newcomers and the weight of the institutional norms protected the institutional sexism of the House of Commons, at least for the first years of the new Labour government.

Behavioural Change

The next step is to show that women MPs act on their support for sex equality. Does this difference translate into identifiable behavioural differences between women and men MPs? Did women try to achieve institutional change? Here the answer is more positive. Although it may not be fair to expect consistent and major change to result from the 1997 increase in British women representatives, it is fair to question what the women have tried to do. Since 1997 Sarah Childs (2004a) has been doing just that. She interviewed new Labour women MPs to ask them, amongst other things, what they tried to do and what they thought they achieved. Childs assessed whether women MPs 'acted for' women and whether they had a different style of politics to men.

She found that many of the new women MPs expressly sought to represent women. Moreover, they believed that they succeeded. They drew attention to their accomplishments in debates, in Select Committees and in the use of Early Day Motions. They reported their use of such opportunities to intervene as Parliament offered (Childs 1999, 2001; Childs and Withey 2005). Childs's MPs also thought that they substantively represented women in their constituency work. They pointed out that there were many matters on which 'people would prefer to come and talk to a woman MP'. There were also many issues that women constituents would not speak about to a man, such as forced marriages, domestic violence and health matters (Childs 2001). Childs's work does not yet include male comparators against which to test these assertions. However, her important point is that the new women MPs believed they represented women. They argued that Labour women raised women's concerns in Parliament and had an effect on policy on violence against women, on childcare and on equal opportunities.

These self-assessments are not shared by all observers of Parliament. During the first Labour government, the new women MPs were not believed to be effective by sections of the press, by other politicians and by many feminist activists. The vote to cut lone parent's benefit in 1997, in which only one of the 65 new Labour women rebelled, was a defining moment. They were thereafter pilloried in the press, by members of the opposition and by many advocates of equality policy. The response of the women loyalists was that rebellion was not an effective parliamentary strategy. Fiona MacTaggart and others claimed that the demands made by women MPs on behalf of the lone parents were met. However, they were achieved later and were the result of behind-the-scenes activities. MacTaggart and others claimed that their lobbying ensured that the cut was in effect restored by the Chancellor in the following budget. The restoration got considerably less press attention than the vote on the original cut (Childs 2004a; MacTaggart 2000).

This example illustrates the possibility that women politicians prefer to work through lobbying, bargaining and compromise. The argument made by women MPs is that behind-the-scenes politics is more effective than outright rebellion (Childs 2004a). In other words it is *better* politics. Their defence is contested. Whilst there is some agreement that outright rebellion may not be a particularly effective way to get things done, and that backbench MPs do have a bargaining position, it is not necessarily the case that behind-the-scenes activity works. Indeed, promises made in such transactions may be a way of taking advantage of the in-experience or ambivalence of women MPs (Cowley 2002). Moreover, basic democratic conventions of transparency and accountability are strained by the adoption of political strategies that do not take place in public.

Overall, the 1997 intake of Labour women MPs were less likely than other groups to rebel in roll call votes. Their loyal voting behaviour cannot be washed way from the statistics by controlling for experience, region or attitudes (Cowley 2002). But the case that they have a different political style remains unproven and perhaps unprovable (Childs 2001; Childs and Cowley 2003).

Policy Change

How then may we assess the claim of the new Labour women that they do politics differently? There is a growing literature on this issue. For example, in their study of Early Day Motions between 1997 and 2001, Childs and Withey report evidence of effective interventions by women MPs on women's issues (Childs and Withey 2005). There is also evidence of policy change. The 1997–2001 Labour government adopted a number of policies in areas of women's interests. Examples include increased provision for breast screening in the NHS, a national childcare strategy and changes in policies on policing and treatment of violence to women. We cannot be certain that such measures would not have been passed anyway. Equally, one could argue that the things that did not happen should be thought of as evidence of the ineffectiveness of the women representatives. The government was criticized for failure in a number of areas known to be of special concern to women. For example, not only has it failed to use the 'Ministry for Women' properly, in addition it did not institute an effective equal pay strategy, or state provision of full coverage of the costs of childcare. Such failings might be taken as evidence that women were not being represented.

But neither should we ignore the reports by British women MPs that they act for women, empathize with women and provide access to women who previously would not have approached their male MP with problems about domestic abuse or healthcare. While such self-reported influence and effectiveness is not conclusive evidence of women making a difference, it points in the same direction as accounts of women representatives in other legislatures and assemblies both in the UK and in other systems (Duerst-Lahti and Kelly 1995; Mackay 2001; Thomas 1994).

Elsewhere in Britain the evidence is similarly mixed but may be more positive. Fiona Mackay and her colleagues (Mackay et al. 2002) found that women activists had a significant impact on shaping the agenda of the new institutions in the devolved assemblies. Their study describes how women members of the Scottish Parliament were able to enhance the access of women's organizations by the new legislature in the post-devolution period. Their findings show how the processes of securing outcomes that are beneficial to women may raise fundamental issues about the nature of democracy. According to this research, the inclusion of women raises wider issues about the very nature of inclusion as new institutions for consultation and decision-making are established and developed. Mackay's work on Scottish councillors reveals a similar pattern to the one found by Childs at Westminster. Mackay details how elected women believe they have a responsibility to act for women by raising such issues as childcare, domestic violence and equal opportunity issues in policy debates (2001: 114).

Research on the behaviour of women representatives at Westminster and elsewhere may not be conclusive, but it is consistent. A significant body of research indicates that women politicians are more likely than their male colleagues to involve themselves in the promotion of women's concerns (Carroll 1985; Duerst-Lahti and Kelly 1995; Haavio-Mannila et al. 1985; Vallance and Davies 1986). Some studies suggest that women may have a different political style. The 1995 collection of essays about legislators in the USA edited by Duerst-Lahti and Kelly (1995) offers a wealth of evidence that political style is gendered. Survey and interview evidence indicates that women politicians prefer the politics of problem-solving, policy development and service delivery to the politics of confrontation. Some research indicates that women MPs have a more caring and collaborative style than men (Norris and Lovenduski 1995). These findings are consistent with earlier studies, e.g. by Norris (1987), which find that women place a higher priority on social issues that relate to family, children and women than do men (see also Haavio-Mannila et al. 1985; Thomas 1994). In short, the balance of the available evidence is that women are likely to intervene to place women's concerns on the political agenda. Finally, there is some evidence that the presence of women legislators strengthens democracy by increasing the political participation of women. For example, in Britain in 2001 women's voting turnout was 4 per cent higher than men's in seats in which a woman was elected to Parliament. Moreover, women reported that they were more interested in the electoral campaign and more likely to be active in seats where a woman MP was elected (Norris et al. 2004). Similar results were found in American studies (Burns et al. 2001).

Examples

One of the very rare British cases in which it is clear that a decision was influenced by women representatives was the Sex Discrimination (Electoral Candidates) Act, which received royal assent in 2002. As described in chapter 5, this is an example of change that is difficult to understand or explain without consideration of the increased number of women representatives and the processes that brought them into the legislature. Women MPs lobbied repeatedly for this change, supported by women activists in the Labour Party and also by advocacy organizations such as Fawcett. It is difficult to see how the Act could have been passed without the work of women MPs, without the efforts of party activists and without the skill of women's advocates. It was a process in which women MPs were amongst the central players. It suggests that by 2001, when the bill was proposed, Labour women MPs had acquired the skills to make changes in a system that was not particularly hospitable to them.

A contrasting example is the House of Commons modernization process. This is an example of an issue on which the support of women MPs, arguing on grounds of women's interest for a measure, was considered to be a disadvantage. It is a long story. The issue of parliamentary modernization was on the agenda by the time of the 1997 general election. During the 1990s, parliamentary reform in general and Commons reform in particular was discussed in the press in articles, editorials and letters to the editor from private citizens. Public opinion polls included items on reform. Civic organizations and the business community were very active in lobbying government on reform. The debates were framed in terms of the nature and future of democratic institutions. Differences between women and men were discussed within that frame. The themes were modernization and democratization.

The problem was that Parliament was thought to be inefficient (took a long time to pass bills), old fashioned (worked according to practices devised for the nineteenth century) and not particularly successful at scrutinizing government. As one scandal after another was brought to public attention, government was routinely criticized for its over-centralization and lack of democracy, while Parliament was in turn criticized for its failure to hold government to account.

Inevitably, the arcane practices of Parliament made for arcane debates that were important but with implications often comprehensible only to insiders. A Parliamentary Modernization Committee, chaired by Leader of the House Anne Taylor, met after 1997. The committee was cautious and its reforms were limited, to the disappointment of many reformers. Women MPs who advocated family-friendly hours were not treated seriously. As I have already described, when new Labour women MPs called for major changes, they were accused by the press and by other politicians of being interested only in improving their own working conditions and not in the onerous work of being an effective representative.

After 2001 the modernization agenda was advanced when Robin Cook became Leader of the House of Commons. Cook, a long-standing reformer, was anxious to modernize. He put forward a number of proposals, including various measures to streamline procedures and make the Commons more efficient, including changing the hours of work, reforms to debate procedures, timetabling, the carry-over of bills from one session to the next and time limits on MPs' speeches. Proposed changes to parliamentary working hours proved very controversial. Prior to the reforms, debates frequently continued beyond the 10 p.m. finishing hour and, until the 1997 Parliament, often went on into the small hours of the morning. These brutal working hours had been the subject of criticism for years.

Those who favoured change argued that the public was entitled to the best attention their MPs could give. *The Times*, for example, argued that the current system led to the routine scheduling of important decisions at late hours when 'everyone involved is mentally unfit to make them and no one else is up to hear that they have been made' (<times.online.co.uk>, 30 October 2002; accessed 11 April 2003). It was argued that normal hours would be more democratic and efficient, more family-friendly, better suited to the media, better for the health of MPs and better suited to the modern era. Those who were against the reform argued that the changes would further marginalize Westminster, make MPs look lazy, diminish the effectiveness and importance of committee work and create a metropolitan elite of those MPs whose constituencies were near Westminster. Opponents, including some Labour backbenchers, believed the reforms would further increase executive power at the expense of the legislature. Older MPs (few in number – more than half of the Commons has experience only of Blair as Prime Minister and only 7 per cent were MPs when Mrs Thatcher was Prime Minister) such as Gwyneth Dunwoody drew attention to the powers that had been lost by Parliament. In short, the debate was framed in a complex set of arguments in which concern about democracy and accountability was crosscut by considerations of professionalization and representation. Divisions between and among women and men MPs of the various political parties from northern and southern regions made it difficult to characterize the issue in either conventional political terms or in terms of gender.

Nevertheless, issues of women's political representation were part of the mix of arguments that informed the modernization debates. For some women MPs the debate and discussion around women's underrepresentation rapidly slipped into discussions about the barriers to women that current parliamentary practice presented (Lovenduski et al. 2005). The issue of the parliamentary culture and its brutal and family-hostile working hours and practices were highlighted by many Labour women MPs. As discussed above, Labour MP Tess Kingham stood down at the 2001 general election because it was impossible to combine being a mother to her children with the demands made on an MP. Her view, shared by many, was that evening hours of business, and especially frequent late-night sittings, were unnecessary. Many commentaries about Commons reform made reference to its likely impact on women. Both Joan Ruddock, former Minister for Women, and Barbara Follett, the founder of EMILY, were at the forefront of demands for a more family-friendly parliamentary regime.

Although sympathetic, those responsible for organizing the vote on hours believed that explicit reference to gender dimensions of the reforms might cost them the support necessary to get the new arrangements through. As a result, they tried to play down the family-friendly arguments of some supporters.[2] Even so, MPs aired the issue of family-friendliness during the debate. For example, Caroline Flint said that the late Commons hours affected family life and that she did not wish to return to her family at weekends too exhausted to be a good mother to her children. Oona King drew attention to the need for MPs to fulfil their family responsibilities. The views of the family-friendly proponents were widely reported in the media. Ironically, the Conservative broadsheet, *The Daily Telegraph*, noted that at one point during the discussion of hours there were only two women Conservative MPs on the opposition benches, drawing attention to the very low representation of women among Conservative MPs.

2 Information from Meg Russell to the author. Personal communication.

On a free vote (that is, free of formal party whipping) the proposals were accepted. Provision was made to rationalize the hours by shortening the 12-week summer break and abolishing late-night sittings. The vote drew an exceptionally large turnout of MPs. There was a great deal of behind-the-scenes activity by supporters and opponents of reform. According to *The Times*, 'whoops of joy' by women MPs greeted the announcement of the result, an indication of their support for the reform.

Part of the argument for the reform was to do with family-friendly working hours, but women MPs were enjoined by reform advocates not to make their case in feminist terms in case such a discourse lost the support of members of the House who were scornful of the new women. The example offers an indication of how strong was the resistance to the women 1997 entrants, not only from the press but also from other politicians, both women and men in all parties. This resistance is an important example of what Yoder (1991) referred to as a surge effect when women enter gender-inappropriate occupations. Reluctance to use arguments framed in feminist terms was an important after-effect of the post-1997 backlash against women MPs.

What Else Happens When the Numbers of Women Change?

The metaphors of backlash and surge indicate that resistance to women 'space invaders', whilst intense, may be temporary. We might imagine that as time passes the presence of women would be normalized and accepted. There are two senses in which to ask if such optimism is justified. First, will women representatives eventually be accepted as normal? Second, however, will such normalization be evidence of assimilation or will it mean transformation as politics is regendered?

To answer, we may consider what has happened in systems where women's representation is better and longer established.

Swedish experience suggests an answer to the first question. In the Swedish Riksdag, procedures and cultures were more welcoming to women and the numbers of women deputies increased much earlier. They continued to rise and are now near equality. Women made up 14 per cent of Swedish deputies by 1971 and passed the 30 per cent mark in 1985. In 2003 they constituted 45 per cent of Riksdag deputies; by 2004 they were campaigning for 50 per cent of the seats. Swedish women politicians are a normal part of the landscape and have been for generations.

Some recent research suggests that the process of normalization is associated with increases in the numbers of women. In her excellent study of women representatives in Belgium and Sweden, Mercedes Mateo-Diaz argues that while their presence remains below or around 15 to 20 per cent of the legislature, women MPs are less like women voters than male MPs are like men voters in terms of their social characteristics. The difference is due to distortions caused by political recruitment processes that were designed to select suitable men. In such processes, when women are recruited, they have to display male qualifications; hence, they will tend to have social characteristics more likely to be found among men. For example, they may have careers in male-dominated professions such as business or law. Alternatively, they may have sacrificed their domestic lives in order to compete in male-dominated arenas and thus would share social characteristics with neither women nor men. For example, they may be less statistically likely to marry or to have children than other women. However, as the proportion of women nears parity, it becomes more likely that women are selected because of their gender rather than despite their sex, and as a result they are more likely to reflect the social characteristics of women in the electorate (Mateo-Diaz 2002).

This observation brings me to the second question. Does normalization mean women MPs are assimilated or is it an indicator of transformation? A growing body of research reports that the attitudes of women and men gradually converge as the numbers of women increase. This and similar findings have alarmed sex equality advocates (see Karvonen and Selle 1995). The fear that women representatives have been assimilated, have become more like men, is very strong. Because it is difficult to design research that illuminates the directions of such change, it has not been possible to answer the second question. However, recent research gives reasons for optimism. Mateo-Diaz (2002) found evidence that, as the balance between men's and women's presence is achieved, women representatives have more influence on the attitudes and preferences of men politicians than the other way around. Her findings add to a growing body of evidence that one of the things that changes as the numbers of women change is men. The process of claiming presence for women both generates and is part of a wider reconsideration of gender roles that itself alters gender regimes. Thus we should expect to find new patterns of political behaviour whereby not only do women and men politicians *become* more similar, but also, as generations shift, politics attracts and recruits men and women who *are* more similar.

To return to the language introduced in the introductory chapter, the question of how, if at all, equality of women's representation leads to changes in political institutions needs to be considered in the context of concurrent institutional changes. The idea of the 'lag' effect illuminates how political institutions are able to insulate themselves from change. Established systems may be poorly equipped to accept changes in gender regimes. However, changes in personnel and recruitment procedures mean that such insulation may be predicted to be temporary, even if long lasting.

British evidence bears out the 'lag' hypothesis. Women's presence has increased throughout decision-making institutions, a pattern also visible in other EU states. It is harder to assess whether the presence of more women is an indication that institutions are 'shrinking'. Certainly, the alterations in state capacities and sites of decision-making described by Banaszak and her colleagues (2003) indicate weakening in institutions of democracy and accountability. An analogous point is made by David Judge when he writes that the growth of 'governance', with its array of appointed bodies, affects the quality and personnel of representation and makes it more difficult for citizens to hold government to account (Judge 1999: 121). On the basis of these readings, increases in women's presence may coincide with declining importance of representative institutions.

The UK, one of the countries most resistant to change, is a tough case. Yet this closed political system with its unfavourable electoral rules and traditional culture of masculinity now has substantial numbers of women in most of its elected and appointed political institutions. Since 1997, structural, procedural and agenda changes have occurred in which gender effects are explicitly highlighted and discussed. Gendered shifts in discourse have accompanied political regime change. The focus of debate shifted from why there should be more women in Parliament to how to get them. The description of the Labour Party modernization process in chapter 5 illustrates important changes in political parties. The Labour Party is experiencing a change in its gender regime whereby the allocation of resources, the division of labour and the structure of emotional attachments of men and women are altered.

British politics itself has also changed. During the years since 1997, changes in the political environment have become evident. The policy agenda has widened to increase the attention given to such issues as domestic violence, childcare, family life, women's health and political representation. Senior politicians, including the Prime Minister, have taken parental leave, a clear signal that the government thinks that personal fulfilment is important and that domestic responsibilities should be shared by both partners. Senior women politicians openly call themselves feminists. By the time of the debates on the Sex Discrimination (Election Candidates) Bill in 2001 and 2002, it was generally accepted that there should be more women in politics. In Scotland and Wales the number of women in both legislatures rose in the 2003 elections, demonstrating that once women incumbents were in place, they were able to maintain their presence. Access to government by women's organizations has improved and women's advocacy organizations have expanded their capacity. Thus the process of increasing women's representation has apparently influenced the issue agenda and altered political discourse. Old-fashioned institutions, although still male-dominated, offered sites of organization for feminist politicians. The feminization of politics continues. It is likely that there will be continued change in a sequence of mobilization, claiming, progress, backlash and defeat, in a cycle that will be repeated for some time to come.

Conclusions: Why Should Women Representatives Make a Difference?

As argued in chapter 2, considerations of justice are enough to support the increased representation of women. Women do not have to make a difference to merit inclusion. But we nevertheless expect them to and fear they may not. It has often been argued that pioneer women legislators became surrogate men, were socialized into the legislature and became indistinguishable from the men they replaced. When I asked my students why they thought some men were so resistant to having more women in politics, they said it was because men behave differently when there were no women present and some men really like being able to do that. On such reckoning, the presence of even one woman will alter men's behaviour and the presence of several will alter it more. However, the only certain presence effect is the disruption or discomfort caused by the arrival of people who are thought to belong somewhere else.

Despite this, expectations of new women representatives are high and often unrealistic. Such expectations come from a number of political communities and are used by resistors to presence in their assessments of achievements. Thus critics such as political journalists, who know perfectly well how

Parliament works, pretend to expect women MPs to be roll call rebels. They do this in order to establish a basis for criticisms that would otherwise be difficult to make. Other politicians pretend they do not know that it takes years to find out how Parliament works. On this basis they claim that the new women MPs understood the nature of the institution they were joining and therefore should not complain about the unnecessarily long hours. Such behaviour is in the theatrical, exaggerated nature of the Westminster political show. We do not expect governments to change their minds about policies when the Prime Minister is savaged by the Leader of the Opposition at question time. We no longer expect governments to resign even when they lose votes in the House of Commons. But such events are reported, discussed and framed in terms that pretend that we do. These are the daily rituals of British political life.

The set of obligations that women MPs picked up in the course of campaigns for inclusion increased their responsibilities as politicians. Expectations that new Labour women MPs would rebel were accompanied by assumptions that they would be advocates of other equalities. Such assumptions are a product of the inclusion politics in terms of which feminists often make their claims. They are portended in feminist writing where there is a frequent implication that women's struggle for equality has the potential to effect equality and inclusion for all excluded groups. Arguments for presence of one group open the way for claims of presence to be made by other excluded groups. Such claims resonate with feminists both on grounds of equity and on difference.

Failure to give sufficient attention to the claims of other excluded groups, particularly ethnic minorities, is one of the many criticisms made of women's mobilization to achieve representation. The criticism frequently, but not exclusively, comes from advocates of 'black' equality who argue that women's equality of political representation is in practice equality only for white women. According to Labour Party Chairman Ian McCartney, the replacement of male incumbents by women candidates for the 2004 local elections was controversial and contested by black advocacy groups. Speaking at the launch of the Electoral Commission's report on Gender and Political Participation on 27 April 2004, McCartney described the difficulties of requiring long-serving male councillors to stand down in order to create vacancies for women. In some areas, minority ethnic councillors were replaced by white women because no minority women came forward to be selected. Although minority communities were enjoined to nominate women, the practice led to charges that the policy was racist and to arguments that more women politicians meant fewer minority ethnic politicians. Charges of racism thus combine with the logic of the politics of inclusion to increase the pressure on women representatives who thereby acquire responsibility for all excluded groups.

This chapter has shown that both the arguments to increase women's representation and the contexts in which they are made seem to promise not only change but also transformation. Although substantive and descriptive representation are analytically distinct, there is a tendency to expect substantive representation to follow from descriptive representation. Moreover, because gender identities ascribe to women a different style of politics, they are expected to transform institutions. Claims are frequently made in the arguments for representation that women's interests and ways of doing things will affect political life profoundly. Broadly speaking, the arguments for presence have raised expectations that culture, discourse and policy will change to a more gender-balanced equilibrium and that incoming women will pave the way for further increases in women's presence.

In short, if the question of what difference women will make is not justified, it is inevitable. It may ultimately be unanswerable. Women enter political life during wider processes of change that mask causality. Much of real-life political bargaining is obscure, unrecorded and subject to numerous interpretations. So we cannot be sure that the increased presence of women has led to one change or another. But we can observe processes and participants and we can also ask women representatives what they think they have done and what they think others have done. We can, as I have in this book, consider what else is changing when the numbers of women are changing and we can also trace processes of change and offer circumstantial evidence in support of a case that women bring change.

Almost all the systematically collected empirical evidence indicates that feminizing politics is accompanied by other changes. But with so few balanced legislatures on which to test our expectations, the case remains unproven. We cannot be absolutely sure that women representatives are making a difference, only that a difference is being made and they are part of the process. We can show that an issue on the feminist agenda has been given attention and that women MPs participated in bringing that issue forward. Many of the effects of increasing women's representation are embedded in the political process.

Viewed in the abstract, feminizing politics is like many other political processes. If feminization is a cause of change, it is also a result of it. When examined closely, particular changes cannot be attributed to any individual. The causes of policy change are notoriously difficult to assess. It is almost impossible to show why a particular decision was made. As one of the MPs who spoke to Sarah Childs remarked: 'You can't say we have changed that but you can say we've worked six weeks on that and . . . change has come about' (Childs 2001).

The observations, evidence and arguments offered in this book suggest that quite a lot of changes accompany women's growing presence in politics. Although no proof so far offered is scientifically conclusive, study after study finds differences in attitudes between women and men politicians, especially in attitudes to sex equality. If no direct, irrefutable, causal relationship between women's presence and the pursuit of women's interests has been discovered, a substantial amount of circumstantial evidence nevertheless connects women's presence to policies that address women's concerns.

References

Abdela, L. (1989) *Women with X Appeal*. Bristol: MacDonald Optima.

Acker, J. (1992) 'Gendered institutions: from sex roles to gendered institutions', *Contemporary Society* 21.

Allwood, G. and Wadia, K. (2000) *Women and Politics in France: 1958–2000*. London and New York: Routledge.

Ashley, J. (2002) 'Can the media be re-sexed?' in J. Lovenduski, R. Campbell and J. Sampson-Jacent (eds.), *Women, Public Life and Democracy*. London: Pluto Press.

Baker, P. (1984) 'The domestication of politics: women and American political society 1780–1920', *American Historical Review* 90.

Baldez, L. (2004) 'Elected bodies: the adoption of gender quota laws for legislative candidates in Mexico', *Legislative Studies Quarterly* 29(2).

Banaszak, L. A., Beckwith, K. and Rucht, D. (eds.) (2003) *Women's Movements Facing the Reconfigured State*. Cambridge: Cambridge University Press.

Bashevkin, S. (1998) *Women on the Defensive: Living Through Conservative Times*. Chicago: University of Chicago Press.

Baudino, C. (2005) 'Gendering the republican system: debates on women's political representation in France', in J. Lovenduski, C. Baudino, M. Guadagnini, P. Meier and D. Sainsbury (eds.), *State Feminism and the Political Representation of Women*. Cambridge: Cambridge University Press.

References

Bergqvist, C. et al. (eds.) (1999) *Equal Democracies? Gender and Politics in the Nordic Countries.* Oslo: Scandinavian University Press.

Bird, K. (2003) 'Who are the women? Where are the women? And what difference can they make? Effects of gender parity in French municipal elections', *French Politics* 1.

Black, N. (1989) *Social Feminism.* Ithaca NY: Cornell University Press.

Bologh, R. (1990) *Love or Greatness: Max Weber and Masculine Thinking: A Feminist Enquiry.* London: Unwin Hyman.

Brooks, R., Eagle, A. and Short, C. (1990) *Quotas Now: Women in the Labour Party.* London: Fabian Society Tract 541.

Brown, A. (2000) 'Designing the Scottish Parliament', *Parliamentary Affairs* 53.

Brown, A., Donaghy, T., Mackay, F. and Meehan, E. (2002) 'Women and constitutional change in Scotland and Northern Ireland', *Parliamentary Affairs* 55.

Burns, N., Schlozman, K. and Verba, S. (2001) *The Private Roots of Public Action.* Cambridge, MA: Harvard University Press.

Buxton, F. (2001) *Electing More Women MPs for the Conservative Party.* London: Bow Group Pamphlet.

Campbell, B. (1987) *The Iron Ladies.* London: Virago.

Carroll, S. (1985) *Women as Candidates in American Politics.* Bloomington, IN: University of Indiana Press.

Caul, M. (1999). 'Women's representation in parliament: the role of political parties', *Party Politics* 5(1).

Childs, S. (1999) 'Revisiting women's political representation'. Paper presented at *EPOP Annual Conference.* University College, Northampton. September.

Childs, S. (2001) 'In their own words: New Labour women and the substantive representation of women', *The British Journal of Politics and International Relations* 3.

Childs, S. (2004a) *Women Representing Women: New Labour's Women MPs.* London: Frank Cass.

Childs, S. (2004b) 'A feminised style of politics? Women MPs in the House of Commons', *The British Journal of Politics and International Relations* 6(1).

Childs, S. and Cowley, P. (2003) 'Too spineless to rebel? New Labour's women MPs', *British Journal of Political Science* 33(3).

References

Childs, S. and Withey, J. (2005) 'Sex and the signing of Early Day Motions in the 1997 Parliament', *Political Studies.*

Cockburn, C. (1991) *In the Way of Women: Men's Resistance to Sex Equality in Organisations.* Basingstoke: Macmillan.

Colley, L. (2000) 'Little Havens of Intimacy', *London Review of Books,* 7 September.

Connell, R. (1987) *Gender and Power.* Cambridge: Polity.

Coote, A. and Campbell, B. (1987) *Sweet Freedom.* Oxford: Blackwell.

Cowley, P. (2002) *Revolts and Rebellions: Parliamentary Voting Under Blair.* London: Politicos.

Cram, L. (1994) 'Women's political participation in Greece since the fall of the colonels: from democratic struggle to incorporation by the party-state?' *Democratization* 1(2).

Dahlerup, D. (1988) 'From a small to a large minority: women in Scandinavian politics', *Scandinavian Political Studies* 11.

Dahlerup, D. (1998) 'Using quotas to increase women's political representation', in D. Dahlerup, *Gender Quotas in a Comparative Perspective.* Geneva: ECPR Research Session Report, September 2002.

Dahlerup, D. and Freidenvall, L. (2003) 'Quotas as a fast track to equal political representation for women: why Scandinavia is no longer the model'. Paper presented to the 19th International Political Science Association World Congress. Durban, South Africa, 29 June–4 July.

Davies, C. (1994) 'The Masculinity of Organisational Life'. Paper presented at the Conference on Women and Public Policy, Erasmus, University of Rotterdam.

Delmar, R. (1986) 'What is feminism?' in J. Mitchell and A. Oakley, *What is Feminism?* Oxford: Blackwell.

Duerst-Lahti, G. and Kelly, R. M. (eds.) (1995) *Gender Power, Leadership and Governance.* Ann Arbor: University of Michigan Press.

Eagle, M. and Lovenduski, J. (1998) *High Time or High Tide for Labour Women?* Fabian Pamphlet 585. London: The Fabian Society.

Fawcett (2003) *Conservative Candidates – Where are the Women?* London: The Fawcett Society.

Fawcett (2004) *Liberal Democrat Candidates – Where are the Women?* London: The Fawcett Society.

References

Ferguson, K. (1984) *The Feminist Case Against Bureaucracy*. Philadelphia: Temple University Press.

Footit, H. (2002) *Women, Europe and the New Languages of Politics*. London: Continuum.

Ford, L. E. (2001) *Women and Politics: The Pursuit of Equality*. New York: Houghton Mifflin Company.

Fox, J. (1998) *The Langhorne Sisters*. London: Granta.

Freedman, J. (2001) *Feminism*. Milton Keynes: Open University Press.

Freeman, J. (1975) *The Politics of Women's Liberation*. New York and London: Longman.

Freeman, J. (2000) *A Room at a Time: How Women Entered Party Politics*. Boston: Rowan and Littlefield.

Gaspard, F., Servan-Schreiber, C. and Le Gall, A. (1992) *Au Pouvoir Citoyennes! Liberté, égalité, parité*. Paris: Seuil.

Graves, P. M. (1994) *Labour Women: Women in British Working Class Politics 1918–1939*. Cambridge: Cambridge University Press.

Guadagnini, M. (2005) 'Gendering the debate on political representation in Italy: a difficult challenge', in J. Lovenduski, C. Baudino, M. Guadagnini, P. Meier and D. Sainsbury (eds.), *State Feminism and the Political Representation of Women*. Cambridge: Cambridge University Press.

Haavio-Mannila, E. et al. (eds.) (1985) *Unfinished Democracy: Women in Nordic Politics*. Oxford: Pergamon Press.

Hall, P. (1986) *Governing the Economy: The Politics of State Intervention in Britain and France*. New York: Oxford University Press.

Harman, H. and Mattinson, D. (2000) *Winning for Women*. Fabian Pamphlet 596. London: The Fabian Society.

Hearn, J. (1989) *The Sexuality of Organisation*. London: Sage.

Htun, M. A. and Jones, M. P. (2002) 'Engendering the right to participate in decision making: electoral quotas and women's leadership in Latin America', in N. Craske and M. Molyneux (eds.), *Gender and the Politics of Rights and Democracy in Latin America*. New York: Palgrave.

IDEA (1998) *Women in Parliament: Beyond Numbers*. IDEA.

IDEA (2002) *The Implementation of Quotas: Asian Experiences*. Quota Workshop Report Series. Stockholm: Sweden.

IDEA (2003) *The Implementation of Quotas: Latin American Experiences*. Quota Workshop Report Series. Stockholm: Sweden.

References

Inglehart, R. and Norris, P. (2003) *Rising Tide: Gender Equality and Cultural Change Around the World*. Cambridge: Cambridge University Press.

Jenson, J. (1990) 'Representations of difference: the varieties of French feminism', *New Left Review* 180.

Jones, K. (1993) *Compassionate Authority: Democracy and the Representation of Women*. New York: Routledge.

Kanter, R. M. (1977) 'Some effects of proportion of group life: skewed sex ratios and responses to token women', *American Journal of Sociology* 82.

Kaplan, G. (1992) *Contemporary Western European Feminism*. London: Allen and Unwin.

Karvonen, L. and Selle, P. (eds.) (1995) *Women in Nordic Politics: Closing the Gap*. Hants: Dartmouth.

Kellner, P. (1997) 'Why the Tories were trounced', in P. Norris and N. Gavin (eds.), *Britain Votes*. Oxford: Oxford University Press.

Keswick, T., Pockley, R. and Guillaume, A. (1999) *Conservative Women*. London: Centre for Policy Studies. <http://www.cps.org.uk/women.htm>.

Kingham, Tess (2001) 'Cheesed off by willy jousters in a pointless parliament', *Guardian*, 20 June 2001, p. 16.

Krook, M. L. (2003) 'Gender quotas: a framework for analysis.' Paper presented to the General Conference of the European Consortium for Political Research. Marburg, Germany, 18–21 September.

Lewis, J. (ed.) (1987) *Before the Vote Was Won: Arguments For and Against Women's Suffrage 1864–1896*. London: Routledge and Kegan Paul.

Lister, R. (1997) *Citizenship: Feminist Perspectives*. Basingstoke: Macmillan.

Lovenduski, J. (1986) *Women and European Politics*. London: Harvester.

Lovenduski, J. (1997) 'Gender politics: a breakthrough for women?' *Parliamentary Affairs* 50(4).

Lovenduski, J. (1998) 'Gendering research in political science', *Annual Review of Political Science*.

Lovenduski, J. (1999) 'Sexing political behaviour in Britain', in S. Walby (ed.), *New Agendas for Women*. Basingstoke: Macmillan.

References

Lovenduski, J. (2001) 'Women and politics: minority representation or critical mass?' *Parliamentary Affairs* 54(4).

Lovenduski, J. and Norris, P. (1993) *Gender and Party Politics*. London: Sage.

Lovenduski, J. and Randall, V. (1993) *Contemporary Feminist Politics*. Oxford: Oxford University Press.

Lovenduski, J. and Norris, P. (2003) 'Westminster women', *Political Studies* 51(1).

Lovenduski, J., Baudino, C., Guadagnini, M., Meier, P. and Sainsbury, D. (eds.) (2005) *State Feminism and the Political Representation of Women*. Cambridge: Cambridge University Press.

MacDougal, L. (1997) *Westminster Women*. London: Vintage.

Mackay, F. (2001) *Love and Politics*. London: Continuum.

Mackay, F. (2003) 'Women and the 2003 elections: keeping up the momentum', *Scottish Affairs* 44 (summer).

Mackay, F., Meehan, E., Donaghy, T. B. and Brown, A. (2002) 'Women and constitutional change in Scotland, Wales and Northern Ireland', *Australasian Parliamentary Review* 17.

MacTaggart, F. (2000) *Women in Parliament: Their Contribution to Labour's First 1000 Days*. London: Fabian Society.

Maguire, G. E. (1998) *Conservative Women: A History of Women and the Conservative Party, 1874–1997*. Basingstoke: Macmillan.

Mansbridge, J. (1999) 'Should blacks represent blacks and women represent women? A contingent Yes', *Journal of Politics* 61.

March, J. G. and Olsen, J. P. (1989) *Rediscovering Institutions: The Organizational Basis of Politics*. New York: The Free Press.

Mateo Diaz, M. (2002) 'Are women in Parliament representing women?' PhD thesis. Louvain, Université catholique, Belgium.

Matland, R. and Montgomery, K. (eds.) (2003) *Women's Access to Political Power in Eastern Europe*. Oxford: Oxford University Press.

Matland, R. E. and Studlar, D. (1996) 'The contagion of women candidates in single member district and proportional representation electoral systems: Canada and Norway', *Journal of Politics* 58(3).

Meehan, E. (1985) *Women's Rights at Work*. Basingstoke: Macmillan.

Meier, P. (2005) 'Belgium', in J. Lovenduski, C. Baudino, M. Guadagnini, P. Meier and D. Sainsbury (eds.), *State Feminism and the Political Representation of Women.* Cambridge: Cambridge University Press.

Murray, R. (2003) 'Was the low number of women elected to France's National Assembly in 2002 indicative of the failure of parity as a policy?' MRes dissertation. Birkbeck College, London.

Nelson, B. and Chowdhury, N. (1994) *Women and Politics Worldwide.* New Haven, CT: Yale University Press.

Norris, P. (1987) *Politics and Sexual Equality: The Comparative Position of Women in Western Democracies.* Boulder, CO: Lynne Rienner.

Norris, P. (1996) 'Women politicians: transforming Westminster?', in J. Lovenduski and P. Norris (eds.), *Women in Politics.* Oxford: Oxford University Press.

Norris, P. (1999) 'The gender-generation gap', in G. Evans and P. Norris, *Critical Elections: British Parties and Voters in Long Term Perspective.* London: Sage.

Norris, P. (2000) 'Gender and contemporary British politics', in C. Hay (ed.), *British Politics Today.* Cambridge: Polity.

Norris, P. (2004) *Electoral Engineering.* Cambridge: Cambridge University Press.

Norris, P. and Lovenduski, J. (1995) *Political Recruitment: Gender, Race and Class in the British Parliament.* Cambridge: Cambridge University Press.

Norris, P. Lovenduski, J. and Campbell, R. (2004) *Gender and Political Participation: The Activism Gap.* London: The Electoral Commission.

Oakley, A. and Mitchell, J. (eds.) (1997) *Who's Afraid of Feminism? Seeing Through the Backlash.* London: Hamish Hamilton.

Pateman, C. (1988) *The Sexual Contract.* Cambridge: Polity.

Perrigo, S. (1996) 'Women and change in the Labour Party', *Parliamentary Affairs,* January.

Phillips, A. (1995) *The Politics of Presence.* Oxford: Oxford University Press.

Phillips, A. (1999) *Which Equalities Matter?* Cambridge: Polity.

Pitkin, H. F. (1967) *The Concept of Representation.* Berkeley: University of California Press.

Pugh, M. (1992) *Women and the Women's Movement in Britain 1914–1959.* Basingstoke and London: Macmillan.

Putnam, R. (1993) *Making Democracy Work.* Princeton, NJ: Princeton University Press.

References

Puwar, N. (2004) 'Thinking about making a difference', *British Journal of Politics and International Relations* 6(1).

Randall, V. (1982) *Women and Politics*. Basingstoke: Macmillan.

Rhodes, R. (1995) 'The institutional approach', in D. Marsh and G. Stoker (eds.), *Theory and Methods in Political Science*. Basingstoke: Macmillan.

Russell, M. (2000) *Women's Representation in UK Politics: What Can Be Done Within the Law?* London: The Constitution Unit, UCL.

Russell, M. (2003) 'Women in elected office in the UK, 1992–2002: struggles, achievements and possible sea-change', in A. Dobrowolsky and V. Hart (eds.), *Women, Politics and Constitutional Change*. London: Palgrave.

Russell, M., Mackay, F. and McAllister, L. (2002) 'Women's representation in the Scottish Parliament and the National Assembly for Wales: party dynamics for achieving critical mass', *Journal of Legislative Studies* 8(2).

Sainsbury, D. (1993) 'Sweden', in J. Lovenduski and P. Norris (eds.), *Gender and Party Politics*. London: Sage.

Sapiro, V. (1981) 'When are interests interesting? The problem of political representation', *American Political Science Review* 75.

Savage, M. and Witz, A. (eds.) (1992) *Gender and Bureaucracy*. Oxford: Blackwell.

Shepherd-Robinson, L. and Lovenduski, J. (2001) *Women Candidates in British Political Parties*. London: Fawcett.

Short, C. (1996) 'Women and the Labour Party', *Parliamentary Affairs* 49(1).

Squires, J. (1999) *Gender in Political Theory*. Cambridge: Polity.

Squires, J. and Wickham-Jones, M. (2004) 'New Labour, gender mainstreaming and the Women and Equality Unit', *British Journal of Politics and International Relations* 6(1).

Stephenson, M. (1998) *The Glass Trapdoor: Women, Politics and the Media During the 1997 General Election*. London: Fawcett.

Stetson, D. McBride (2002) 'Introduction: abortion, women's movements and democratic politics', in D. McBride Stetson (ed.), *Abortion Politics and the Democratic State: A Comparative Study of State Feminism*. Oxford: Oxford University Press.

Thomas, S. (1994) *How Women Legislate*. Oxford: Oxford University Press.

References

Vallance, E. (1979) *Women in the House: A Study of Women in Parliament.* London: The Athlone Press.

Vallance, E. and Davies, E. (1986) *Women of Europe: Women MEPs and Equality Policy.* Cambridge: Cambridge University Press.

Vogel, U. (1988) 'Under permanent guardianship: women's condition under modern civil law', in K. B. Jones and A. Jonasdottir (eds.), *The Political Interests of Gender.* London: Sage.

Vogel, U. (1994) 'Marriage and the boundaries of citizenship', in B. Van Steenbergen (ed.), *The Condition of Citizenship.* London: Sage.

Wängnerud, L. (2000) 'Testing the politics of presence: women's representation in the Swedish Riksdag', *Scandinavian Political Studies* 23(1).

Ware, A. (1996) *Political Parties and Party Systems.* Oxford: Oxford University Press.

Webb, P. (2000) *The Modern British Party System.* London: Sage.

Welch, S. and Studlar, D. T. (1996) 'The opportunity structure for women's candidacies and electability in Britain and the United States', *Political Research Quarterly* 49(4).

Yoder, J. (1991) 'Rethinking tokenism: looking beyond numbers', *Gender and Society* 5(2).

Young, I. M. (1996) *Justice and the Politics of Difference.* Princeton: Princeton University Press.

Index

Acker, Joan, 48
Afghanistan: quota system, 96
Agacinski, Sylviane, 132
all-women shortlists, *see* AWS
Arab countries: quota systems,
  102
Argentina: quota system, 94,
  102
Armstrong, Hilary, 121
Ashley, Jackie, 154
Astor, Nancy, 40, 49
AWS (all-women shortlists),
  115–21, 127; and Sex
  Discrimination Act, 120

Badinter, Elisabeth, 132
Baker, Paula, 35
Bangladesh: quota system, 94
Belgium, 174; quota system,
  103
Bennett, Catherine, 155
Bird, Karen, 131
Blair, Tony: and AWS, 119;
  takes parental leave, 176

'Blair's Babes', 4–5, 154, 155;
  see also House of Commons,
  women in
bodies: and civil society, 25–6,
  27–8, 33; politicization of,
  42; women's, to be
  controlled, 33–4
Bolivia: quota system, 102
Bondfield, Margaret, 40
Boothroyd, Betty, 55–6, 155
Botswana: quota system, 94
Brazil: quota system, 102
Brennan, Ken, 26
Brinton, Helen, 154
Britain: legislation affecting
  women, 37; 'Ministry for
  Women', 112, 113, 161,
  162, 163, 167; political
  institutions, 26, *see also*
  House of Commons; politics
  and change, 176–7, 179–80;
  quota system, 94, 105,
  106–7, 136, *see also under*
  Labour Party; women's

political representation, 1,
4–6, 7–8, 9, 10, 15, 22,
41–2, 43–4, 46
Brittain, Vera: *The Honourable
Estate*, 1
Brooks, Rachel, 113
Brown, Gordon, 114
Buxton, Fiona, 152

Campbell, Bea, 39
candidates, parliamentary: and
selection procedures, 66–80;
obstacles facing women,
75–81; selection of women
as, 1, 66–8, 69–75, 81, 82,
107, 115–17; 121–3, 124,
130, *see also* quota systems
Carlisle, John: sexist comments
by, 55
Carlton, Anne, 119
CEDAW (Convention on
the Elimination of
Discrimination Against
Women), 102
Childs, Sarah, 6, 165, 180;
*Women Representing
Women*, 4
Chirac, Jacques, 132
citizenship: as male-only, 24,
25, 27; and women's
representation, 22
Cobbe, Frances Power, 34
Coleman, Peter, 114
Colley, Linda, 5
Commission for Equality and
Human Rights (Britain), 163
Conservative Party (Britain):
and devolution, 123, 124;
hostility of to women MPs,
49; ideology of, 59–60;

opposed to quotas, 128;
selection of candidates by,
69–72, 81, 82, 130; sexism
in, 77, 80; and women voters,
23, 60, 89, 150, 151–2; and
women's interests, 39, 172;
women's section in, 38
Contagious Diseases Acts, 34
Cook, Robin, 170
Co-operative Women's Guild,
39
Costa Rica: quota system, 94
coverture, 24
'critical mass', 141, 142,
143–4
Cryer, Ann, 5

Dahlerup, Drude: theory of
'minority representation',
144, 159
Davies, Celia, 51
democracies: citizenship
in, 22; quotas and, 102;
representative, 16
demographic change, 7
domestic violence, 34–5
Drown, Julia, 156
Dunwoody, Gwyneth, 171

Eagle, Angela, 113
East Timor: quota rejected,
97
Eastern Europe: quotas,
103; women's political
representation, 87, 100–1
electoral systems, 106;
differing impact of, on
women's representation, 47,
98–100, 117
EMILY, 115

Equal Opportunities
  Commission (EOC), 40, 161
equal opportunities policy, 4
Equal Rights Amendment
  (USA), 42–3
equality (of political
  representation): arguments
  for, 21, 22–5, 31; and
  ethnic minorities, 178–9;
  guarantees of, 91; promotion
  of, 90–1; rhetoric of, 90, 92
European Union:
  Constitution of, and
  women's representation,
  87; electoral system, 106

Fabricant, Michael, 27
Fawcett, Millicent, 36
Fawcett Society, 19, 65, 127,
  153
feminism: and concept of the
  political, 13; definitions
  of, 28–9; 'difference' and
  'equality' strands of, 2–4,
  6, 29–36, 43; and ethnic
  minority claims, 178–9; and
  political parties, 38, 40–1,
  88, 89, 106–7, 136–9; and
  reform, 41–2, 44; and
  temperance movements,
  35; and women's interests,
  19–20, 141; *see also*
  Women's Liberation
  Movement
Flint, Caroline, 172
Follett, Barbara, 115, 172
Footit, Hilary, 6
Ford, Lynne E., 6
France: electoral system,
  130–1; *parité*, 131–6; quota

systems, 94, 102–3, 103,
  105, 130–1, 133; women's
  political representation,
  41–2, 131–2, 133–4 & table
  5.5, 135–6
Freedman, Jane, 6
Freeman, Jo, 39, 88, 89

gender: and behavioural codes,
  51; and difference, 24–5;
  gap, 149–53; importance of
  as political issue, 10; and
  political parties, 59, 63,
  137–9, 159, *see also under
  individual parties*; and
  political style, 23, 28, 144,
  156, 168–9, 174–5, 179,
  see also House of Commons,
  culture of; v. sex, 20–1; and
  US politics, 43, 149; and
  voting patterns, 149–52, 169
gender relations: changing, 7,
  96, 145, 175; and social
  difference, 24
Gibson, Anne, 119
Gorman, Teresa, 55
Greater London Authority
  (GLA): electoral system,
  106, 126
Greece, 137
Green Party (Britain), 43
Guillaume, Angela, 152

Harman, Harriet, 112, 162,
  163
Hearn, Jeff, 54
Hewitt, Patricia, 150, 162, 163
House of Commons (Britain):
  culture of, 26–7, 46–8,
  49–50, 54, 56, 146–9, 164,

178; electoral system for, 106; hostility of to women MPs, 49, 55–6, 147, 155–6; modernization of, 169–73; women in, 4–6, 31, 54–5, 147–9, 153–6, 158–9, 160–4, 165–7, 177–8
House of Lords: women appointees to, 126

institutions, political: backlash against women, 153–6, 173, *see also* media, vilification of women MPs by; and change, 84, 165–6, 175–7, 179–80; creation of gender-balanced, 83–4; and democracy, 16; and gender, 26, 28, 50–1, 140, 145–6, *see also* masculinity, institutional; reform of, 84, 165–6; sexism of, 46–8, 50–6, 75–80, 143; *see also* House of Commons; parties, political
Iraq: quota system, 96
Italy: quota system, 103

Jay, Margaret, 162, 163
Jospin, Lionel, 132
Jowell, Tessa, 162
Judge, David, 16, 176
Juppé, Alain, 132
justice: of women's representation, 22, 89–90, 177

Kanter, Rosabeth Moss, 142, 143, 159
Keswick, Tessa, 151–2

King, Oona, 172
Kingham, Tess, 156, 172
Kinnock, Neil, 111, 115
Kosovo: quota system, 96

Labour Party (Britain): and AWS, 115–16, 118–21; changes in, 176; class-based ideology of, 60–2; and feminism, 163; quota systems for women in, 9–10, 66–7, 68–9, 107, 112, 113–24, 126–7, 129–30; selection of candidates by, 66–8, 81, 82, 107, 115–17; 121–3; sexism in, 77, 80, 117; and OMOV, 116; and trade unions, 108–9, 109, 110, 111, 116; women MPs in, 4–6, 117 & table 5.1, 153–4, 159, 160–1, 165–7, 167–9, 169–70; and women voters, 150–1, 152; and women's interests, 39, 107–8, 110; and women's representation issues, 43, 61, 112; women's sections in, 38, 61, 66, 108
Labour Women's Action Committee (LWAC), 112, 115
Labour Women's Network (LWN), 113, 115
Lait, Jacqui, 162–3
Latin America: quota systems, 100
Liberal Democrat Party (Britain): ideology of, 62; selection of candidates by,

Liberal Democrat Party
(Britain): (*cont'd*)
72–5, 81, 82, 124, 130;
opposed to quotas, 127;
and women's representation
issues, 62–3
Liberal Party (Britain): and
women's representation
issues, 43; *see also* Liberal
Democrat Party
Lincoln, Deborah, 114, 119
Lister, Ruth, 24, 25, 26, 27–8

McCartney, Ian, 178–9
Mackay, Fiona, 6, 56, 168
MacTaggart, Fiona, 166
Manufacturing, Science and
Finance Union (MSF): and
OMOV, 116
marriage: women's
disadvantaged legal status in,
34, 35
Married Women's Property
Act, 34
masculinity: institutional,
26–7, 46–8, 49–52, 53–4,
146–7, 164; of political
parties, 57–8, 63–4
Mateo-Diaz, Mercedes, 174
Mattinson, Deborah, 150, 151
May, Teresa, 70, 128
media: vilification of women
MPs by, 5–6, 154–5
Mennen, Carlos, 103
Morgan, Sally, 127, 162, 163
motherhood: politicized, 35–6
Mussolini, Alessandra, 103

Norman, Matthew, 154
Norris, Pippa, 98, 99, 150

OMOV (one member one
vote), *see* Labour Party,
and OMOV

Pakistan: quota system, 94, 102
parité, *see* France, *parité*
parties, political: ideologies
of, 59, 63; and selection of
women candidates, 1–2,
38–9, 64–77, 80–2, *see also*
quota systems; and sex
equality, 159–60; and
women politicians, 40,
128–9 & table 5.4, 144–5;
and women's claims to
representation, 56–8, 59–63,
92; women's sections in, 38,
39; *see also* feminism, and
political parties; *individual
political parties*
Pateman, Carole: *The Sexual
Contract*, 20, 24
Pfeiffer, Emily, 36
Phillips, Anne, 22, 141
Pitkin, Hannah, 16
Plaid Cymru: quota system of,
124
Pockley, Rosemary, 152
political institutions, *see*
institutions, political
political parties, *see* parties,
political
political representation, *see*
representation, political
politics: defined, 12, 13;
feminization of, 12–14,
176–7, 179–80; male-
dominated, 13; style of,
and gender, 23, 28, 144,
156, 168–9, 174–5, 179

positive action, *see* equality,
  promotion of
positive discrimination, *see*
  equality, guarantees of
power: women excluded from,
  1–2, 7, 8, 27
Prescott, John, 114
'presence' (women's), 140,
  141–2, 143, 177, 179, 180;
  in legislatures, 156–8, 158–9,
  165–9, 179–80
private sphere: politicization
  of, 32–3, 35–6; women
  relegated to, 25, 27–8, 34,
  52
public v. private spheres,
  25–6, 33, 34; and double
  standards, 34; *see also*
  private sphere
Puwar, Nirmal, 48, 147–9

quota systems (for women
  candidates), 9–10, 66–7,
  68–9, 92–104, 107, 136;
  efficacy of, 96, 98–9, 138–9;
  fast-track, 100; forms of,
  94; legality of, 120, 126,
  127; opposed, 96–8; and
  strategies, 101–4; supported,
  95–6; worldwide, 93, 94–5,
  96, 100, 102–3, 105–7,
  123–4, 128, 130–1, 136;
  see also Labour Party, quota
  systems for women in;
  France, *parité*

Race Relations Act (Britain),
  126
racism, 68, 78–9, 80, 179

representation, political:
  arguments for equality of,
  21, 22–5, 31; descriptive,
  17–18, 179; nature of,
  14–15, 16; and institutions,
  2–4, 5–6, 15, 16, *see also*
  institutions, political;
  substantive, 18, 179;
  see also women's political
  representation
Richardson, Jo, 112, 113
Roche, Barbara, 162, 163
Ruddock, Joan, 55, 162, 163,
  172
Russell, Meg, 123, 127

Scandinavia: women's political
  representation, 7, 8, 9, 97,
  99–100
Scotland: electoral system, 106,
  122; feminist agenda and
  devolved government, 84–5,
  86–7, 121; quota system,
  123–4, 128; women in
  Parliament, 85–6, 97, 125 &
  table 5.2, 128, 153, 168,
  176–7
Scottish National Party (SNP),
  124, 128, 130
Sedgemoor, Brian: sexist
  comments by, 155
sex, *see* gender, v. sex
Sex Discrimination
  (Electoral Candidates)
  Act (Britain), 91, 126,
  127, 169, 176
sex equality: attitudes towards,
  159–60, 180
sexism, 46–8, 50–6, 75–80,
  117, 143, 155, 164

sexuality: Victorian regulation of, 33–4
Sheppard Towner Act (USA, 1921), 37
Short, Clare, 56, 110, 112, 113, 114, 115, 118, 119
Skinner, Dennis: sexist behaviour by, 55
Smith, John, 115, 118
Social Democratic Party (Britain), 43, 109, 111–12
South Africa: quota system, 100, 102
Squires, Judith, 164
suffrage movements, *see* women's suffrage
Sweden: women in politics, 83, 138, 157–8, 174
Sylvester, Jo, 70

Taiwan: quota system, 94
Tanzania: quota system, 94
Taylor, Anne, 170
Thatcher, Margaret, 5–6, 40, 43, 108
Townswomen's Guild, 39
trade unions (Britain): and Labour Party, 109; 111; and women, 108–9, 110, 111, 112, 113
Trades Union Congress (TUC): Equal Rights Unit, 112
Tribune Group, 116
'twinning', 122–3, 124

Uganda: quota system, 96, 102
United Nations: Platform for Action, 90
United States: anti-feminist backlash, 43; Democratic Party and women, 137, 149; gender politics, 43; legislation affecting women, 37–8, 42–3; politicization of domestic sphere, 35; women activists marginalized, 39; women's political representation, 41–2, 88–9

Vogel, Ursula, 24–5

Wales: electoral system, 106, 121, 122; quota system, 123–4, 124, 128; women in National Assembly, 86, 97, 125 & table 5.3, 128, 176–7
Wängnerud, Lena, 157, 158
Webb, Paul, 59
Weber, Max: theory of bureaucracy, 51–2
Whitty, Larry, 114, 118
Wickham-Jones, Mark, 164
Widdecombe, Ann, 155
Wintringham, Margaret, 49
women: activists marginalized, 39–40; and exclusion, 1–2, 7, 8, 20, 46, 52; interests of, 18–20, 157–60; invisibility of, 25, 52, 53; legislation affecting, 34, 37–8, 41; political style of, 168–9, 179; underrepresented worldwide, 45–6; voting patterns of, 37, 38, 115, 149–50, 169; *see also* feminism
Women and Equality Unit (Britain), 163, 164
Women's Liberation Movement, 41, 42

Women's National
Commission (WNC), 161
women's political
representation, 2–4, 7–11,
16, 21; feminism and, 2–4,
13–14, 15, 29–32, 41–4,
47–8, 140; influence of,
165–73; necessity of, 141;
normalization of, 173–7;
and political parties, *see*

parties, political, and women
politicians
women's suffrage, 1, 15, 32,
35, 36–7
Women's Unit, 163–4; renamed,
163; *see also* Britain, 'Ministry
for Women'

Yoder, Janice, 143, 173
Young, Iris Marion, 141